EARLY AMERICA AT WORK

EARLY

A PICTORIAL GUIDE TO

BY
EVERETT B. WILSON

AMERICA AT WORK
OUR VANISHING OCCUPATIONS

New York: A. S. Barnes and Company • London: Thomas Yoseloff Ltd

To

B. B. W.

Introduction

This is a book about our neighbors—both past and present, both good and bad. It is concerned with the names we have applied to them, not their given names or surnames, but the descriptive names that tell us who they are or were, what they do or did, and where they rank or ranked in the social, political, professional, and economic worlds.

A few hundred years back, when our civilization was much less complex—when almost everyone was either a master or a subject—one did not need much of a vocabulary to identify those who lived around him. But in the diversified era in which we live today, we need thousands of names to describe our friends and neighbors.

We need one large group of names when talking about the occupations and activities of our neighbors and another when speaking of their personal characteristics and habits.

We require one set of names when talking about the past and another for the present, because established vocations disappear rapidly, as our economy develops and as automation presses relentlessly onward. And new occupations appear almost overnight, as new developments like electronics and space travel come along.

In addition, the names we apply to continuing occupations change with the years as new names catch on for one reason or another.

Gone completely are such onetime, everyday occupational names as lamplighter, chimney sweep, coachman, and powder monkey. Few people today can identify the fletcher, the webster, the farrier, the snobscat, and the costermonger of Colonial times.

In addition to the full-time vocations, there were scores of part-time occupations for which names were needed. Such rural workers as the hay pitcher, the wheat shocker, and the corn husker performed that work only during the harvest and worked at other seasonal functions during the remainder of the year. The town crier, ice cutter, and oyster peddler also filled other jobs when not working at those specialties. Back on the farm, the spinster, the churner, and the rail splitter turned their attentions to other gainful pursuits when not spinning, churning, and splitting rails.

As for changing names, we still have the amanuensis, but we call her a secretary or stenographer. The horse doctor has become a veterinarian, the sempstress is a dressmaker, the peruker is a wig maker, the seedsman is a florist, and the plumbum worker is a plumber. Literally hundreds of occupations have taken on new names through the years.

On top of all that, the descriptive names and epithets we apply to the human characteristics and habits of our neighbors keep changing with the times, and the new ones all too often lack the sparkle and precision of the older ones. We used to call a fool a doddypoll, a tightwad a pinchpenny, a rascal a rapscallion, and a wise guy a wisenheimer.

The purpose of this book is to recall the old-time occupations and epithets and to picture the neighbors to whom they applied. If it should happen that some of the more colorful names of the past might thereby be revived, thus enriching our vocabularies, spicing up our conversations, and sharpening up our descriptions, so much the better.

It will be noticed that many of the names mentioned herein have meanings other than those discussed, but this is not a dictionary, so there is no need to mention those definitions that do not apply to the subject of the book.

The illustrations were reproduced for the most part from magazines and books published prior to the turn of the twentieth century. Original photographs were taken by the author.

E.B.W.

Bethesda, Md.

Contents

EARLY AMERICA AT WORK

COLONISTS FACING INDIAN ATTACK

1. The Pioneers

Among the first of our vanishing neighbors, not counting the Indians, were the hardy Colonists who settled the eastern shores of the United States and were called Colonials after they became established.

Some of them were the stiff-necked Puritans who eschewed personal pleasures and practiced a rigid moral code; some were Pilgrims, the separatists from their Church who came here to escape religious persecution; some were individuals who sought a better way of life than they could enjoy back home, and others were criminals sent here to get them out of their native lands.

The Pilgrims were so devout and so opposed to frivolity, such as Christmas celebrations, that they spent their first Christmas Day felling trees to build a home for one of their group.

When the Colonists or their descendants decided to move west, they were called pioneers, if they were among the first to populate an area; settlers, if they settled down and started farming; homesteaders or prairie breakers, if they occupied a piece of land offered free by the government to those who would develop it; and squatters or nesters, if they settled down on land owned by someone else, as many did. If they lived on or near the coast, they were coasters; if near the border of a Colony, they were borderers.

Few people answer to these names today, now that our frontier has become civilized and colonies are in disrepute.

Except in Alaska, homesteading is a thing of the past because no more really attractive land is available for the purpose. However, some one million, four hundred thousand homesteads were established in the nineteenth and early twentieth centuries.

The Frontiersmen

Most of the Colonials who went west did so for the purpose of establishing farms and ranches, but others went for different reasons or else changed their minds after they arrived.

There was the hardy adventurer, who went out to the frontier for the thrills he might experience, and there was the prospector—the forty-niner—who went with his grubstake in search of gold and silver, in the hope of striking it rich. There was the fur trader who traded wampum or trinkets, blankets, and other goods to the Indians for furs and pelts, and the hunter or fowler who devoted himself principally to hunting wild game, such as buffalo, deer, wild turkeys, and so on.

People also were known by the sort of place in which they lived, so one could be a mountaineer, a plainsman, a woodsman, or a backwoodsman. Most of them are farmers or ranchers today, but the older terms still are used colloquially.

A newcomer to the West, especially if he were young, shy, or overly citified, was called a greenhorn or tenderfoot and was subject to ridicule and harrassment because of his inexperience.

PURITANS WORKING ON CHRISTMAS

PIONEERS IN COVERED WAGONS

The Indian Fighters

Hostile Indians were a source of great concern to the colonists and pioneers of our country. Scalping parties and massacres were all too common, and people living near the frontier, or in areas which the Indians refused to give up peaceably to the white man, had to be constantly on the alert for sudden raids.

This meant that every family had to keep firearms in the house. Women as well as men knew how to use them, and every male able to handle a bow and arrow or a musket or rifle was subject to service as an Indian fighter. These fighters not only defended their homes and communities but also became members of expeditions sent out to apprehend hostile Indians who had perpetrated a raid on a white settlement and perhaps carried off women and children, as well as horses, oxen and other property.

Knowledgeable woodsmen and friendly Indians acted as Indian scouts, either for the purpose of detecting raiders in advance or locating tribesmen being tracked down after committing crimes. The expeditions sent out after Indians also required Indian guides and pathfinders to show them the way about the country.

The Vigilantes

Self-constituted judicial bodies known as vigilance committees were organized in the early days in the Far West for the protection of life and property when the local authorities were unable to handle the situation or when no such authorities existed. Members of the committees were private citizens who called themselves vigilantes. They dealt with horse thieves, cattle rustlers, renegade Indians, desperadoes, and other criminals. Vigilance committees were active in the Frisco goldfields in 1851 and also in mining towns in Idaho and Montana.

A WAGON-TRAIN GUIDE

A PROSPECTOR

PRAIRIE BREAKERS IN TROUBLE

A FORTY-NINER

17

A MOUNTAINEER AND HIS STILL

BUFFALO HUNTERS

18

A FRIENDLY SCOUT

A SCOUT SOUNDS THE ALARM

INDIAN FIGHTERS

They not only pursued and apprehended the outlaws but also tried them and carried out the sentences if the prisoners were found guilty.

Other groups of private citizens organized to take the law in their own hands in this country have been the Ku Klux Klan, the Knights of the White Camellia, the Pale Faces, and the Invisible Empire of the South, formed to deal out extra-judicial punishment to Negroes and carpetbaggers.

Unofficial justice and punishment also were dealt out to such offending citizens as wife beaters, scolds, and blasphemers by groups of righteous citizens known as regulators, who were active in Colonial days in New England and elsewhere.

VIGILANTES

VIGILANTES STAGE A HANGING

HANGING DESPERADOES

2. The Public Servants

The Burgomasters

There have been numerous changes in the names of public servants and in the functions performed by those who serve their community. The mayor once was known as the burgomaster in some parts of the country, just as free citizens were known as burghers or burgesses.

The individual who issued local currency was a mintmaster. The stamp officer, who administered the hated stamp tax which led to the Revolutionary War, is no longer among us by any name.

In most places, we no longer have the deathsman or Jack Ketch as the hangman was called, other more civilized means of doing away with vicious criminals having been perfected.

The Lamplighters

Before electricity came along, streets and entrances to homes and other build-

A LAMPLIGHTER

ings were lighted by lamps that burned candles, whale oil, kerosene, and, finally, illuminating gas. And because economy was the watchword in those days, this meant that someone had to light the lamps when darkness approached and then douse them when daylight began to return. The individuals who performed this work were called lamplighters.

Depending on the nature of the fuel being used, they did the lighting by means of torches or tapers. Inasmuch as the duties of a lamplighter coincided timewise with those of a town watchman also called a rattlewatch, one man often handled both jobs.

A typical watchman not only kept an eye out for horse thieves, burglars, and other criminals, but also for unfriendly Indians, spies, and hostile troops. His equipment usually consisted of a lantern and a spear or musket, as well as his lighting gear if he had that responsibility.

Through the night, the watchman would call out the hour, the state of the weather, and assurance that "All's well," if indeed that were the case. When an emergency arose, he gave the alarm in his loudest voice.

The Town Criers

Prior to the advent of daily newspapers, radio, telephone, and television, not to mention loud-speaker trucks, getting important information to the general public was no easy matter.

One way used to gain the attention of the populace was to ring a loud,

centrally-located bell, usually a church bell or one located on top of town hall, which would bring the people running to the village square, and that work required a toller or bell ringer.

In addition to summoning the people to church twice on Sunday, church bells often were used to announce the opening and closing of markets and the arrival of ships, to give fire alarms, to mark the death of prominent personages, to call town meetings, and to warn of hostile Indians or other invaders.

A TOWN CRIER

Another way was to send one or more men out to the people, equipped with a small bell, drum, or trumpet to attract attention. Such an individual was called a town crier, herald, or bellman. He would move about town reading a proclamation or message from the author- ities. The town crier also told of missing children, drownings, shipwrecks, lost cattle, and other happenings.

Aside from ringers of town bells and church bells, there were ringers of farm bells and ship bells.

A HERALD

A BELLMAN

A CHURCH DRUMMER

25

A WATCHMAN

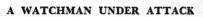

A WATCHMAN UNDER ATTACK

26

The Chimney Sweeps

One of the most picturesque of our vanishing occupations is that of chimney sweep. There are individuals who still call themselves by that name and who perform the function of cleaning chimneys, but the nature of the job is now far different from the days when the heating of homes was accomplished by means of open fireplaces and wood-burning stoves.

The accumulations of soot had to be cleaned out regularly to prevent chimney fires which, in those days of wooden or thatched roofs and frame buildings, some with wooden chimneys, could result in costly fires that might spread to neighboring buildings.

For the most part, the job of chimney sweep was a dirty and lowly one, but when a town suddenly found itself without anyone available to clean chimneys, the job took on new importance, and special inducements were offered to persuade individuals to enter the calling.

The most typical method of cleaning chimneys was to use small boys— and girls—who could climb up inside and loosen the soot with small brooms and other tools and by the passage of their bodies. Small men also used to perform the job but, regardless of age, the work presented serious hazards to health and personal well-being. Considering that no one bathed too often in those days, it is easy to see how the person of a chimney sweep might get into really bad condition.

Some home owners would tie a white goose on the end of a rope and collect soot by running it up and down the chimney. The chimney sweep finally disappeared as a result of the passage of child labor laws and other legislation designed to protect the health of individuals so engaged.

A CHIMNEY SWEEP

Thos. Kent 1900

The Viewers

If it sometimes seems that we have an excessive number of inspectors, it may help to recall that we used to have numerous others that have been discontinued, while some have taken on new names.

Gone entirely are the hog reeve and the hayward or field driver, officials who dealt with stray hogs and cattle respectively in the wide-open days when animals of either type were likely to get into cultivated fields or come strolling down Main Street. The hog reeve was charged with seeing that loose hogs had rings in their noses and were properly marked.

The ratcatcher now is an exterminator, while the dogcatcher is becoming known in progressive communities as an animal warden, a name presumed to carry greater dignity. Thus, we may cease hearing the expression, "He couldn't be elected dogcatcher," sometimes said of a political candidate deemed to have little standing with the voters, and indicating also that dogcatcher is one of the lower ranking political jobs.

The early-day community also had a variety of people, often called viewers, who served as inspectors. Not heard of these days are the chimney viewer or fire warden, who inspected kitchens for unsafe conditions and looked after chimneys that needed to be cleaned out or were made of unsafe materials; the cat inspector, who dealt with stray and diseased felines; and the gutter viewer, who watched for roof gutters that spilled rain or snow water on passersby.

The egg viewer, who looked for bad eggs, is an egg candler today. The func-

EGG VIEWERS

tions of the weight viewer and the gager, who tried to detect merchants who gave short weight or short measure, have been combined in the inspector of weights and measures. The fence viewer, who checked the condition of the fences around the town common or pasture, is gone, and the crowner or corpse viewer is a coroner.

The tide waiter, so called because he had to wait until the tides would permit ships to dock, is a customs inspector, and the scrutineer has come to be called an election judge or poll watcher.

A HOG REEVE

The Law Enforcers

Keeping the peace and apprehending criminals was as much of a problem in the early days as it is now. Every town had a judge who often was referred to as a beak. The law enforcement officer, whom we call the sheriff, used to be known as a shrieve. Though the sheriff remains, we no longer hear of the posse, which was a group of private citizens, usually mounted on horses, summoned by the sheriff in an emergency to go out after a horse thief or other fugitive.

A detective or plainclothesman was a sleuth, sleuthhound, or spotter, while a jailer was a gaoler or turnkey.

The officer we today call a policeman, copper, or cop had a variety of names, one of the most popular being constable. Others were tipstaff, catchpole, bang beggar, leatherhead, flatfoot, bull, and peeler.

SPOTTERS

A GAOLER WITH HIS KEYS

The Cops on the Beat

The foot patrolman, who once pounded his beat in his long brass-buttoned overcoat and round helmet, twirling his nightstick, flirting with the girls, and filching an occasional apple from the fruit stand, is almost a thing of the past. The policeman on foot can still be seen in downtown areas, but in residential sections his modern counterpart is found in a squad car or prowl car, sometimes on a motorcycle.

The homeowner and storekeeper, who always used to chat with the patrolman as he strolled down the street, probably

A PATROL WAGON

A BRAVE CONSTABLE

A BLACK MARIA

do not even know the name of the officer in the squad car today. That does not mean they are not getting good protection from the police. Thanks to the auto and the two-way radio, the protection is better than ever.

Because traffic moves so much faster, there have been other changes. The horse-drawn patrol or paddy wagon, known in some places as a Black Maria, and its foot gong have given way to the motorized patrol car with its siren. Gone, except in a few larger cities, are the mounted police, whose towering horses have been replaced by motorcycles, and the bicycle cops, who used to apprehend bicycle speeders in the old days.

The Whitewings

The street sweeper, who used to clean the streets in a white uniform back in the days when the horse was king, was known as a whitewing. He not only cleaned up after the horses, a very necessary function in those days from a sanitary point of view, but also swept up trash and debris. If he lacked a white uniform, he was known as a street cleaner or mudlark.

His equipment consisted of a wide brush with a long handle, a broom, a wide-mouthed scoop or shovel, and a large can mounted on wheels so he could push it along the street. In winter when there was snow on the ground, the wheels were replaced by runners.

Today, with the horse out of the pic-

ture, the street cleaner is becoming a novelty, especially in residential areas where mechanical sweepers are taking over.

A WHITEWING

A LEATHERHEAD

A ROUNDSMAN

The Snow Wardens

Another worker in the streets was the snow warden. In the Northern States, sleds and sleighs used to replace wheeled vehicles whenever a good snowstorm came along, because they could be pulled about much more easily. But when everyone changed over, it was necessary to keep the streets covered with a layer of snow because the runners of the sleds and sleighs did not do well on bare spots caused when the wind blew the snow away or when thaws began.

Thus, the snow warden had a double job. One was to pack down the snow with the aid of a huge, wooden, horse-drawn roller wherever it became too deep. The other was to throw snow on the bare spots and on covered bridges so the runners would move more easily. Wooden snow ploughs pulled by one or two horses were used to remove excess snow in the streets and sidewalks in the days before motorized equipment and chemicals came along to do the job.

In larger cities, a half dozen or more horses were hitched to huge plows, and in rural areas a dozen oxen often were hitched up to "break out" a road blocked with deep drifted snow.

A SNOW ROLLER

3. The Itinerants

The Wanderers

Until more modern transportation facilities were devised, the itinerants—those people who habitually moved about the countryside—had a choice of going on foot, on horseback, in a horse-drawn vehicle, or on a boat.

Travelers who went on foot were divided into several distinct groups. There were the peddlers of goods, the providers of services, the foot travelers journeying to a specific destination, and the wanderers who had no real objective other than a change of scenery and free meals and lodgings.

If the walkers were on the seamy side, they were called tramps, rovers, vagabonds, viators, or hobos. The name hobo has come to mean a tramp who travels by railroad, free-of-charge, on or under freight cars.

Tramps, who usually carried their meager belongings with them in a sack, thrown over their shoulder or on the end of a stick, were not above petty thievery. Dogs barked at them, and children were warned by their parents to keep a safe distance.

More often than not, they were accomplished beggars who sought handouts but shunned work of any kind. If a householder offered food in return for work, such as chopping wood, a tramp sometimes reluctantly agreed but then left a mark on a gate or tree warning other tramps of his unfortunate experience at that home.

Other itinerants who walked to a destination instead of riding were known as footers, farers, wayfarers, roadsters, peregrinators, or pilgrims. The latter name applied also to people who devotedly traveled to a holy place.

Today, walking any distance has almost become a lost art. The counterpart of yesterday's walking itinerant either buys a jalopy, takes a bus, or gets about by hitchhiking. The genuine tramp, proceeding on foot, has become a rare sight.

The Peripatetics

Among the professional people who traveled by horseback or horse and buggy were the peripatetic preacher, the peripatetic physician, the peripatetic judge, and the peripatetic school teacher, although the latter usually was more of a tutor than a classroom instructor.

Typical peripatetics served a group of

A WAYFARER AT REST

A TRAMP AFTER A FREE MEAL

communities, repeating the circuit from time to time. They moved about because there was insufficient population or financial inducement to justify their remaining in one place continuously.

A peripatetic judge also was known as a circuit rider. We still have our circuit court judges but they no longer move about via horsepower, and our clergymen who serve several neighboring parishes simultaneously are no longer called peripatetics.

There also were peripatetic authors, artists, and naturalists, who often ranged far afoot in the pursuit of their professions, living off the land or the generosity of their admirers along the way.

The Peddlers

In the days when most people lived on farms, often some miles from the nearest town, they obtained many of their everyday requirements from peddlers, who brought the goods to them, instead of taking the time and trouble to go to town by horse and wagon or carriage, assuming they owned such equipment.

The highways and byways were full of peddlers of all descriptions. They were known as hawkers, hucksters, duffers, foggers, foot-goers, jugglers, packmen, storewagon men, riverboatmen, or traders. They differed from the vendor

A PEREGRINATOR   A FOOTER

ROADSTERS WASHING UP

who remained in one place or in a restricted area where he displayed his wares on a cart or stand, and they were unlike the traveling salesman of today in that they carried their wares with them and delivered them on the spot, whereas the salesman carries samples and takes orders for future delivery from a factory or warehouse.

The old-time peddler transported his wares either in a trunk or knapsack that he carried on his back, in saddlebags if he rode a horse, or in a cart, wagon, or boat. If he called out his wares to attract customers, as was commonly done in well-populated areas, he was referred to as a hawker or huckster. And if he lacked a suitable voice or did not speak good English, he sometimes hired a professional crier to do his hawking for him, just as wealthy individuals sometimes used to hire professional weepers to perform at the funeral of a relative or public figure. Some peddlers used a trumpet or a bell to attract buyers as they rode down the street.

Peddlers sold almost every kind of movable commodity used by the public. They were most ingenious at condensing a maximum quantity of merchandise into a limited space, especially if they traveled on foot with their wares on their back or in a small wagon.

The foot peddler usually was obliged to confine himself to small, light items, such as needles and pins, hooks and eyes, razors and razor strops, scissors, knives, spoons, combs and brushes, mats, lace, shoelaces, spectacles, drugs, perfume, spices, dyes, incense, buttons, beads, hats, caps, pencils, pens, soap, matches, tobacco and cigars, snuff boxes, and small hardware.

Every fraction of a cubic inch had to count in a peddler's pack. A tin pot might be filled with buttons and beads or tobacco. A snuff box would be filled with needles and pins. There was not a void of any consequence in the pack of an experienced peddler.

The fact that some unscrupulous peddlers, who never expected to see their customers again, sometimes deceived the public by passing off wooden nutmegs and oak-leaf cigars helped to give all peddlers a bad name. Though some were known as honorable and reliable individuals, peddlers as a class were noted for deceit and trickery. They had a reputation for being cunning and impudent and completely unscrupulous. *Caveat emptor* was a sound rule to follow when dealing with peddlers in those days.

There is good evidence that local storekeepers had something to do with the bad reputation that attached to peddlers. Since every dollar spent with a packman was one dollar less to be spent at the crossroads store, it was only natural that the less scrupulous store owners would try to discredit their competition. In some places, storekeepers joined together in persuading the authorities to require peddlers to obtain a license and to restrict the types of merchandise they could sell.

Peddlers fortunate enough to have carts or wagons could, of course, handle heavier and bulkier goods, such as Bibles, almanacs, wooden clocks, cotton and woolen goods, axes, paint, nails, hammers, woodenware, neckerchiefs, shawls, pottery, tinware, brooms, boots, shoes, carpet slippers, glassware, pots, firearms, washboards, rolling pins, looking glasses, and items of clothing. They supplied a large percentage of the goods that farm and town folk purchased from others.

A CIRCUIT RIDER

A PERIPATETIC PREACHER

The peddler either was a self-employed individual or the employee of a small manufacturer, such as a maker of tinware. His stock of goods was obtained from small producers in town or taken in trade from farmers and their wives, who traded articles they made in their spare time for things they needed but could not make. Indeed, trades were much more common than cash transactions.

A peddler often would start out with a load of miscellaneous merchandise, which he would trade for furs or other items as he went along; and then, in turn, would dispose of the goods he had taken in trade at some distant town; sell his horse and wagon, and return to his starting place by boat or stage. There he would acquire a new stock, buy another horse and vehicle, and begin all over again.

A peddler who made a practice of taking goods in exchange for his wares was known as a trader and, if he traded goods such as beads and trinkets or wampum to Indians for furs, he was a fur trader.

Those peddlers who specialized in selling to townspeople often carried a single line, such as fruits and vegetables, religious tracts, fish, and the like. The peddler of books was called a colporteur or bookhawker.

If they used river boats to carry their wares, peddlers were called storeboat-men. They had small retail stores built on rafts or barges and sold their goods as they floated down the river to its mouth, tying up briefly at each landing as they came to it. At their destination, the river mouth, when the stock had been disposed of, they usually sold the boat for the lumber in it, then went back up the river, built a new boat, assembled a new stock, and repeated the process.

A later variation of the peddler was the candy butcher, who sold sandwiches, magazines, cigars, or picture postcards, as well as candy, on railroad trains, either while the train was stopped at a station, in which case he had to be adept at getting off the train at the last moment after it started to move, or between stations. In the latter case, the butcher would ride back and forth between two towns, replenishing his stock as needed.

A PERIPATETIC PHYSICIAN

A PEDDLER AND HIS WAGON

A PERIPATETIC ARTIST

A PEDDLER WITH HIS HORNBLOWER

A MILK PEDDLER

A DUMBBELL PEDDLER

Still another type of peddler, who flourished briefly not so long ago, was the bootlegger, who peddled illegal liquor. He is found today only in so-called dry areas, having been eliminated elsewhere by repeal of Prohibition.

Salesmen sometimes are called peddlers today, just as they used to be known as bagmen, chapmen, drummers, or commercial travelers, but the term is a misnomer. Genuine peddlers who carry their stocks with them are becoming quite rare.

The Itinerant Servicemen

Just as it was not convenient for rural folk to journey to town for the goods they needed, it also was not convenient to go there for services, so the peddlers of goods were joined on the roadways by a long list of itinerants who offered a wide variety of services.

Prominent among them was the barber-surgeon-dentist who served in a triple capacity in outlying areas until the advance of science relegated him to

A STOREBOAT PEDDLER

the one calling for which he was best trained, that of cutting hair, shaving faces, trimming whiskers and moustaches, giving shampoos, dispensing tonic, and so on.

There also were various itinerant entertainers, who are dealt with elsewhere.

Among the several types of itinerant educators who ranged the countryside were the fencing master and singing master, the teachers of the violin, harpsichord, and melodeon, and the itinerant lecturer.

Traveling illustrators and artists in-

AN ITINERANT CLOCK-FIXER

A TRAVELING CHROMO-PEDDLER

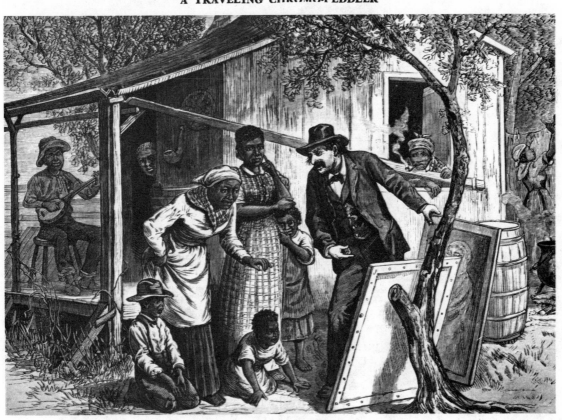

A PERIPATETIC PHRENOLOGIST

AN ITINERANT PHOTOGRAPHER

cluded the daguerreotypist, tintypist, and, later, photographer, who had to use a clamp to keep the customer's head steady during the long time exposures required in those days. There also were the printer who carried his small press in a wagon, and the painter, portrait painter, and profile cutter who made silhouettes to be framed and hung on the livingroom wall.

To aid those unable to do their own weaving were the traveling woolen weaver, chair weaver, and basket weaver. Right on their heels came the cordwainer, who made shoes; the cobbler, soler, or snobscat who repaired shoes in the home, and the sartor or tailor, known to some as a gooseherd because tailors used an iron with a curved handle that resembled the neck of a goose. There also was the indigo peddler whose product was needed to dye wool.

Others who serviced the home were the traveling upholsterer, glazier or windowglassman, wood chopper, candle maker, clock cleaner and clock repairer, phrenologist, and when occasion arose the midwife.

The traveling blacksmith, who brought his anvil and forge in a wagon; the wheelwright who made and repaired spinning wheels as well as wagon and cart wheels; the ratcatcher; the distiller; the tinker or repairer of tinware; the harness maker; the potter, who made pottery; the hooper, who made hoops for casks; the millwheel and tombstone cutter; and the butcher of hogs, cattle, and sheep were others, who made the rounds of farm homes at irregular intervals.

Because they brought with them a fund of gossip and news, not always reliable, which brightened up the dull farm life of those days, the more presentable of these traveling servicemen were welcome visitors in the homes they served. They often received meals, as well as lodging, with the family, as partial compensation for the work they performed.

Of course, other individuals engaged in these same callings had establishments in addition in the larger towns, as is the case today if the need for the service still exists. The piano tuner is one of the few itinerant servicemen who has remained in his original business right up to the present.

A TOOTHPASTE VENDOR

4. The Local Business People

The Street Vendors

Although our towns and cities still have a sprinkling of outside vendors, who sell fruit and other items from street corner stands or from parked trucks, there were many more of them in the days before the supermarket came into being.

These early-day small businessmen and women included the oysterman, gingerbread lady, hot-corn girl, muffin boy, peanut girl, sweet-potato man, and pastryman. There also were vendors of cheese, chestnuts (in the days before the blight killed off our chestnut trees), chickens, fish, honeycombs, hominy, pretzels, pies, and brickdust. The latter was used in the home to sharpen knives.

Each of these vendors had a favored location in which he always could be found.

Some of them had simple wooden stands on which they displayed their wares, while others had small wagons or carts which they rolled each day to a location where crowds were expected to gather, such as a park or beach or ball game. Typical were the popcorn wagon, with its tiny flame to heat the butter, and the peanut wagon, whose owner blew a shrill whistle to remind the public of his presence.

Sometimes these carts were pushed slowly along residential streets to bring the product closer to the consumer, and kids would rush out to make a purchase after wheedling a nickel from papa, just

A SOUP VENDOR

VEGETABLE VENDORS

AN OYSTER VENDOR

as children beg for a dime today to purchase an ice-cream bar from a passing truck.

The Innholders

The roadside inns that dotted the countryside in the days of horse transportation were operated by innkeepers or innholders. If the place was called a tavern, the proprietor was a tavern keeper or taverner. These wayside establishments also were known as ordinaries, run by ordinary keepers; public houses, run by public house keepers, and hostelries, run by hostelers. The

A WAYSIDE INN

keeper of such places also was known sometimes as a Boniface.

The name hosteler is not to be confused with hostler or ostler. The latter were grooms who cared for horses at an inn. Yet a hosteler's mate was a hostler-wife.

An inn, tavern, ordinary, public house, or hostelry sometimes was a rather elaborate two-story building with a large taproom, several ornate parlors, a score or more sleeping rooms, and a commodious stable for the horses. More often, it was a small place with just a few sleeping rooms, and one parlor or none at all, plus a crude shack where horses could be kept overnight. Regardless of size, such a place always had a taproom and a large fireplace at which patrons could dry and warm themselves in inclement weather while they enjoyed a tankard of ale.

Some of the mean little places were run by a man and his wife without even one hostler. Other larger establishments would have several tapsters or tapstresses, known today as bartenders and barmaids, plus a staff of hostlers and grooms, a cellarman to bring supplies up from the basement, and various other servants.

Although their primary function was to provide food, drink, and lodging to travelers, these establishments also served as the local place of entertainment if located near a city or town. Some had billiard tables and large halls where cotillions could be held. Their taprooms served as neighborhood social centers just as many beer parlors do today. Often there was no place else in the vicinity where a resident could go for food, drink, and companionship and to hear the latest news brought by seafarers and other travelers, who were not always reliable news sources.

In remote, sparsely settled regions, trappers and hunters used the taverns as their headquarters and base of operations.

Many of the taverns catered exclusively to the better trade, such as stagecoach passengers and horse traders, who were regarded as being a cut above peddlers, drovers, and waggoners. The latter were encouraged to frequent the

A TAVERN

A COFFEEHOUSE

less pretentious places if there were any nearby.

Some inns were located in towns on main thoroughfares or near a wharf, while others were built at crossroads and ferries out in the country, at points where stagecoaches changed horses or stopped for the night.

When a stagecoach pulled up at a tavern with its load of passengers and baggage, the stage driver would crack his whip loudly to announce the arrival, and the innkeeper would ring a bell to summon the porters and hostlers to tend to the baggage and replace or bed down the horses. Owners of private coaches with their retinue of flunkies also relied on the taverns for food, lodging, and refreshment and received special attention from the innkeeper, in the hope of inspiring generous tips.

Innkeepers felt obliged to accommodate all comers, because travelers had no other place to spend the night. As a result, it often was necessary for three or more people to occupy one bed, although they might be all unknown to each other, and some might be decidedly uncouth or otherwise objectionable.

A SALOONKEEPER WITH TROUBLE ON HIS HANDS

The Coffeehouse Owners

In the larger cities, food and beverages originally were dispensed in coffeehouses, alehouses, and porterhouses, all run by individuals called keepers or owners.

The coffeehouse was a far cry from the hotel coffeeshop of today. In its humble way, it was the first attempt at a restaurant in this country, one of the earliest being the Blue Anchor Tavern which operated in Philadelphia in 1683.

In addition to functioning as bars and restaurants, the coffeehouses, like the wayside taverns, served as informal clubs and meeting places for people of the community, the sort of place where booksellers, literators or literary men, wits, philosophers, and writers of the day "warmed their hearts and loosened their tongues over the steaming cup," as one writer put it.

Sea captains, merchants, and leading citizens also patronized the coffeehouses and enjoyed steaks, kidneys, larks, and oyster puddings, among other delicacies. Some of the places offered gambling as an extra inducement to attract patronage.

The Saloonkeepers

The saloon, which fell into disrepute because of the dubious characters who once patronized it, has all but vanished so far as the name is concerned, but still exists in greater numbers than ever under such names as bar, bar and grill, tavern, and cocktail lounge. The long mahogany bar with its brass rail has vanished in most communities, where it is deemed safer to drink sitting down than standing up. The swinging doors, the darkened windows, the spittoons, the sawdust on the floor, the ladies' entrance, and the nude painting over the bar still are seen in some old-time saloons, but newly constructed drinking places lack such features.

The saloonkeeper now is known as a tavern owner or bar-and-grill proprietor. The free lunch he once served before

Prohibition, either has vanished or has been replaced by a dish of peanuts or popcorn. The always welcome free drink on the house also is a thing of the past in most saloons or successors thereto.

The Merchant Princes

As the present-day type of business structure began to develop after the Civil War, store owners and traders who achieved outstanding success were known as merchant princes. We also used the terms magnate, mogul, nabob, and tycoon to describe men of wealth and position.

A seller of food and supplies to prospectors, settlers, and the like was called a provisioner or chandler, which also meant candlemaker.

An individual who sold provisions and supplies to troops was known as a sutler, victualler, or camp follower. The latter name also applied to a female who consorted with the troops.

MERCHANT PRINCES RELAXING

A RUM DEALER

A SUTLER'S TENT

The owner or manager of a wharf was a wharfinger, the owner of a grist mill or corn mill was a miller, the person who managed a market was a market master, and a steward was a manciple.

A florist was referred to as a seedsman, and a liquor retailer was a rum dealer, since rum was a favorite beverage in the old days, especially in New England where it was distilled from molasses brought back from the West Indies by the trading vessels owned by the merchant princes. A brewer of beer or ale was a maltster or a brewster, if feminine.

A middleman or broker was known as a forestaller. Entrepreneurs, as we sometimes call individuals who assume the risk and management of business, were known as enterprisers and undertakers, the name we use today for a funeral director or mortician.

A MILLER AND HIS HORSE

The Home Craftsmen

The Industrial Revolution, which began in colonial days and has continued ever since, put an end to many small household industries once found in every town of any size and, indeed, on most farms. In colonial days, when factories were unknown, goods sold by peddlers, stores, and trading vessels were made for the most part either in small household shops or in small nearby huts.

The handcraft operation tended to be highly specialized, since one man could turn out only a limited quantity of work without the aid of machinery, and apprentices and journeymen were few in number. Instead of having one organization that turned out finished woolen cloth, for example, each operation often was a separate enterprise.

Before the power and machinery needed to operate a textile factory became available, one's neighbors included carders or combers, who carded or straightened the wool for spinning; the spinners or spinsters, who spun the wool into yarn; the websters, weavers, or warpers, who operated the looms that wove the yarn into cloth; and the fullers, who cleaned and finished the cloth.

The word spinster originally meant spinner and came to be applied to any unmarried woman who, instead of leaving the family to marry and make a home of her own, stayed home with her parents and did the spinning and other family work.

When flax was used in the yarn, there was the flax rippler, who broke off the seed pods, and the flax dresser, hatcheler, hackler, or heckler, who combed out or carded the flax with his hatchel, prior to spinning.

These specialists, mostly women, either worked full-time at their trade or else did what they could after other farm work or housework had been finished. A typical farmwife not only made cloth, called homespun, for her own use, with the aid of her daughters and other female relatives, but also turned out an extra quantity to barter to peddlers and other vendors.

A SPINSTER

A GRIST MILL

The colonial farmer was, and indeed had to be, quite self-sufficient. He bought or traded for such items as salt and iron and metal goods, but produced most of his other needs. He made and traded shoes, gloves, and clothing out of the leather he tanned, and also turned out nails, tools, furniture, casks, shingles, and fence rails.

Carding, spinning, weaving, and fulling, often referred to as the homespun industries, still are necessary in making woolen cloth, but these functions nowadays are performed by factory employees with the aid of machinery. The small independent businessmen of colonial times—the craftsmen and craftswomen known as carders, spinners, weavers, and fullers—have disappeared entirely.

Continuing the woolen goods story, anyone who helped a webster or weaver was a woolen worker, one who removed knots or burls from cloth was a burler, a clothcutter was a shepster, a dyer was a litster, one who raised the nap on the cloth with a thistle was a teagler, those who made the cloth into garments—the tailors of today—were called sartors and fashioners or tailoresses. Cheap ready-

A RIBBON WEAVER

A WEBSTER

64

made clothing was sold in stores owned by slopshop keepers, known also as slop dealers. Their employees were slop workers. Some communities also had ribbon weavers, stocking weavers, silk spinners, and silk throwsters, all of them unknown today.

The same process has taken place in other lines. For example, the bowyer and fletcher who made the bows and arrows used by pioneers have disappeared completely from the classified directory. Their function has been taken over by the sporting goods manufacturer. The armorer, who made the armor used by the Pilgrims and the guns used by colonial hunters and soldiers, has become a small arms manufacturer. The gunsmith now repairs guns instead of making them.

Gone, too, are the glosser and burnisher who polished metal objects in the days of the home craftsman, the plinisher who finished them, the embellisher who decorated the objects, and the gilder who gilded them. Today, this type of work is done in factories by machine.

The Harness Makers

The first step in making leather in the old days was performed by the skinner who removed the skins from the animals. They then were handled by the leatherdresser, currier, or barker who did the tanning.

Aside from boots, shoes, and brogans, leather was used for garments, such as breeches and jerkins, made from deerskin and buckskin. Another user of leather was the harness maker, who did a big business as long as the work horse was on the scene. It was his job to make the reins, checkreins, traces, breeching, bellybands, and other leather parts in a harness. What is left of his work today is done by a saddler.

The shoe repairman, known in the olden days as a soler, snobscat, or cobbler, either did the work in his home, had a shop of his own, or else was an itinerant. The cordwainer, who made shoes to order, either supplied the leather himself or else used hides provided by his customers, who may have produced them on the farm or traded for them in town with a dealer.

If the cordwainer had a considerable volume of business, he had assistants to help with the work, including a binder, stitcher, and laster. An inspector of finished shoes was a sealer. Such a place as a shoe store, with a stock of various styles and sizes of shoes, was unknown until well along in the nineteenth century.

The Turners

Wood was widely used in the early days because it was readily available and easily worked. There was the joiner, now known as a cabinet maker, the nailor, who is called a carpenter, and the turner, who shaped wood with a chisel on a lathe.

A dish turner made piggins, noggins, runlets, kiclers, firkins, buckets, churns, dye tubs, carders, pounding tubs, and the like out of wood.

A COBBLER'S BENCH

A STITCHING HORSE

The roofing applicator, using thatch or hand-made wooden shingles for the most part, was a thatcher, and the dry kiln operator was a clapboard drier. Barrels and casks were made by a cooper, and hoops for barrels were turned out by a hooper.

Logs from which lumber was made were felled in the woods by fellers, axemen, and hewers and cut to size by sawyers. The beam maker converted the logs into beams.

Logs to be used for fencing, preferably chestnut, were split by rail-splitters, and leftover pieces of wood were utilized by whittlers, the old men who sat in front of the general store or close by the potbellied stove and reduced sticks of wood to shavings, just to keep busy, or made simple objects with their jackknives.

The ox-yoke maker has disappeared, along with the oxen which pulled the ox carts or bull carts, ox being the common name for a working bull or steer. The yoke served the same purpose as a horse collar.

The Smiths

Like the modern telephone book, our early towns were full of smiths, as they called workers in metal. We still have silversmiths, locksmiths, and blacksmiths, known also as vulcans, but the others have disappeared. The silversmith continues to make and repair articles made of silver and other metals,

LEATHER BOOTS

SAWYERS

A HEWER

but the modern locksmith repairs locks instead of making them, and the blacksmith is fast giving way to the welder and other competitors.

In the olden days, the blacksmith not only shod horses, oxen, and mules, but also forged the shoes and nails that he used. With the aid of his helper, called a backhander because he stood back of the smith and handed materials to him, the blacksmith made tools, implements, and utensils, such as knives, forks, pots, pans, pothooks, cranes for fireplaces, plowshares, spears, and marking irons for branding animals. He also put iron rims on wheels and repaired objects made of metal.

Aside from his hammers, the blacksmith's equipment included a forge on which he heated the coals, a huge bellows to bring the coals to the desired heat, an anvil on which to hammer the

A LOGGING WAGON DRIVER

A TURNER

metal into shape, and a leather apron to protect him from the intense heat and from the hoofs of the animals he shod.

Today, the electric welder performs the same repair work more expeditiously, the mail order house and hardware store sell the same implements and utensils the blacksmith once fabricated, and the horseshoeing trade has drifted to specialty horseshoers, once known as farriers, who either have a small shop where they fit factory-made shoes or else travel about the country in small trucks or station wagons, calling on their trade, which consists largely of saddle horse and race horse owners.

Other early-day smiths who have lost their identity are the:

axlesmith	ironsmith
bladesmith	knifesmith
boilersmith	pansmith
brassmith	picksmith
clocksmith	platinumsmith
coachsmith	ropesmith
coppersmith	runesmith
goldsmith	scissorsmith
gunsmith	swordsmith
hedgesmith	toolsmith
hingesmith	wiresmith

Their functions continue, in some instances, but under other names.

The worker in tin was called a tin-smith or whitesmith, and the repairer of tinware was known as a tinker, although the latter name eventually came to mean a bungler. The tinner listed in today's classified columns is a sheet metal worker.

The iron master was the owner or operator of a foundry. Other old-time metal workers whom we do not hear of today were the sleighbell maker, bell founder, and bell caster, who made bells for ships, churches, and other buildings; the founder, who now is called a foundryman, turning out cast iron; and the forger, who was not a writer of bad checks—known as a coiner—but a man who worked at a forge, like a blacksmith.

The Mongers

Webster's New International Dictionary lists seventy-two kinds of mongers, a monger being a dealer or trader and often a peddler.

There were alemongers, ballad-mongers, beermongers, bookmongers (also called colporteurs), cheesemongers, clockmongers, coalmongers, clothes-mongers, fashionmongers, fellmongers (dealers in pelts), fishmongers, fruit-mongers or fruiterers, poultrymongers

A WOODCARVER

A BLACKSMITH

A VULCAN

AN OX SLING

A COPPERSMITH

or poulterers, and watermongers. In the days before they had dependable public water systems, peddlers used to sell water from house to house by the gallon or cask.

Also listed in *Webster's* are such improbable persons as bribemongers, lovemongers, meritmongers, phrasemongers, and wordmongers.

The only mongers we hear much of today are the scandalmonger, the scaremonger, meaning alarmist, and the warmonger. Monger has come to imply petty or discreditable dealing in present-day usage.

The Wrights

Another group of early workers included the wrights, meaning workmen, skilled workmen, or craftsmen. Skilled workers also were known as artisans and artificers.

Today we still speak of playwrights and millwrights, but the others, such as the bookwright, gatewright, plowwright, tilewright, and timberwright are heard of no more.

Others who might have been called wrights, but were not, included the spurrier who made spurs, the cutler who made cutlery, the pewterer, who made pewterware, the potter, who made pottery and is today a ceramics manufacturer, and the hatter, who made hats.

The Makers

The suffix -*maker* was added to many words to indicate men who made things.

Among them were the buttonmaker, known also as a button molder, who used bone, ivory, horn, wood, brass, silver, gold, and pewter as his raw materials.

There also was the candlemaker or tallow chandler, who used tallow or grease from such animals as the bear, the deer, the moose, the elk, the ox, and the sheep, to make his products. Candlemaking was another job performed by the farmwife.

One maker whose job disappeared after only a brief period was the paper collar maker. The mantuamaker, who made robes for women, also has vanished.

Other makers included:

blockmaker	hookedrugmaker
broommaker	pillmaker
bucklemaker	potashmaker
chairmaker	powdermaker
charcoalmaker	quiltmaker
clockmaker	shoestringmaker
coffinmaker	sleighbellmaker
combmaker	vinegarmaker
drummaker	snuffmaker
glovemaker	woodenwaremaker

Others, such as shoemaker and bookmaker, continue in our present-day vocabularies.

The Perukers

In Revolutionary times, one very active man was the maker of wigs or periwigs, known as a wigger, wigster, wig dresser, peruker, or *perruquier*. For a time every male who could afford to, in-

A POULTRYMONGER

cluding young boys and children, owned one or more wigs. They were worn for reasons of adornment, as a disguise, to cover up defects of nature, or as a symbol of office. They still are worn by some public officials in England.

Egyptian mummies wore wigs, as did both men and women in the golden days of Greece. In the heyday of their popularity in colonial times, wigs were especially favored by doctors, military officers, clergymen, bishops, and judges.

In Greek theatricals, a person's character was revealed by the color of wig he wore. Red meant a dishonest slave, black indicated a tyrant, and the wearer of a curly wig was recognized instantly as a youthful hero.

Wigs came in all colors and shapes, some reaching to the shoulders and even to the waist of the wearer. They were made from human hair, horsehair, calf hair, cow hair, cotton or wool. It became fashionable to powder wigs and then, when they lost their popularity, people powdered their own hair instead. Today, on the contrary, some individuals spend large sums trying to conceal the fact that their hair has turned gray or white.

A POTTER

A BELLCASTER

The Clipperman

Another extensive list of appellations ended in *-man*. Prominent among them were the clipperman, who sailed on clipper ships; the codman, who helped catch and market codfish; the stallman, who worked in barns with the horses; the catfood man, who had the concession for feeding all the cats in a business district, where they were needed to control the rodents; and the second-hand-meat man, who resold table scraps purchased from restaurants and hotels.

Others were the remittanceman—the black sheep who received a periodic remittance from his relatives on condition that he remain away from home—and the squawman, who married or resided with an Indian woman.

Almost as long was the list of names ending in *-woman*. We still use names such as charwoman and washwoman, known also as a tubwoman or washer-woman, but at one time we had these others:

almswoman	hillwoman
applewoman	journeywoman
boatwoman	lacewoman
chamberwoman	laywoman
chapwoman	leechwoman
coachwoman	oarswoman
dairywoman	packwoman
fieldwoman	playwoman
fruitwoman	shopwoman
gleewoman	tirewoman
herdswoman	waferwoman
wagonwoman	

A chapwoman and a packwoman presumably were female salesmen. A lace-

AN ARMORER

woman was a lady's maid, among whose duties was that of lacing up corsets. A leechwoman was a female physician.

The Sempstresses

Before the day of the clothing factory, the mail-order house, and the specialty clothing store—in fact, until after the Civil War—most clothing was made either by a housewife, a grandmother, a spinster daughter, or an individual called a needlewoman, modiste, sempstress, or seamstress. Known today as a dressmaker, either she went to the customer's home with her needles, pins, thread, thimbles, scissors, beeswax, and tape measure, and did her work in a spare bedroom or parlor, or else had a small shop to which customers brought their material and had their fittings.

The dressmaker, specializing mostly in alterations and repairs, is still with us, although she handles a small fraction of the total clothing business. The factories have taken over the great bulk of the trade.

The draper, who used to sell draperies, fabrics, and upholstery, has become an interior decorator or proprietor of a fabric shop, while the mercer, who dealt in fabrics, is no longer heard of.

Other women workers were the grain-bag mender, the straw-hat weaver, the ribbon weaver, the amanuensis now known as a secretary, and the central,

A TALLOW CHANDLER

A MODISTE

A NEEDLEWOMAN

who once said "Number please," when we lifted the telephone receiver to place a call. She is known today as "operator," but is often replaced by an automatic device.

The Retail Clerks

Most of the vanished or vanishing occupations date from our very early days, but there are exceptions. The automatic pinsetter is in the process of eliminating entirely the agile pinboys, who set up pins in bowling alleys until just a few years ago. The electric golf car and the cart which can be pulled about on wheels have just begun to replace the caddy on the golf course. The caddy is vanishing not only because he has become scarce and expensive, but also because golf course proprietors can make a profit out of renting golf cars and carts, whereas they get nothing out of money paid to caddies by the players.

The automatic elevator is making it possible to dispense with elevator operators even in the largest buildings, and self-service in retail stores is rapidly eliminating the retail clerk who used to fill orders for customers, answer questions helpfully, and carry packages to the door.

Order-filling already has gone almost entirely in the supermarkets. Here self-service has been a success because the shopper visits the store often enough to become familiar with the location of the items she wants and because the management has generously made available carts, in which the customer can move the merchandise about the store. All that are left in these markets are the checkers and shelf-fillers.

Because self-service, which means requiring the customer to assume the order-filling function formerly done by the clerk, means lower payrolls, it has been copied by envious drug stores,

A CHURNER

liquor stores, book stores, and other retail places eager to boost their profits by cutting payroll expense. It is too early to tell whether the public will rebel as this trend expands.

Among unskilled workers who use their hands and backs for a livelihood, the baggage-smasher and baggager have become porters and redcaps. The portress, a female porter, is seldom seen. The docker and hobbler now are known as stevedores and longshoremen.

Gone for good are the chairbearers, who carried women, and men too, from place to place in sedan chairs supported by long poles.

The chiffonier came to be known as a ragpicker, who in turn is called a junk dealer or scavenger. The bulldozer, which can jerk a stump out of the ground before a man can spit on his hands and pick up a shovel, has eliminated the stumpdigger, while mechanical equipment and the increasing

A BOATWOMAN

popularity of other fuels have replaced the coalheaver.

The sandman who once sold sand to housewives to spread on their earthen kitchen floors has long since disappeared, while the dustman is known these days as a janitor. The sandwich man, who carried advertising messages on boards hinged at his shoulder, has been almost entirely replaced as an advertising medium by newspapers, radio, and television, although he still is seen occasionally bearing a message for a striking labor union or a small restaurant.

Among skilled workers, the plumbum worker and lead worker now are called plumbers. We no longer see the razorgrinder, who had a stand on a busy street in the days when men used straight-edged razors; the soft-soap man or soap boiler, who collected grease with which to make soap; the loom-repairer; the churner, who made butter by hand;

A FAN PAINTER

the umbrella-mender, who flourished in the days when umbrellas were used more widely; the bonnet-blocker, who now is called a hat cleaner; or the chair-caner, who filled a need in the days when chairs had cane seats. The bell-hanger who put door bells in place has been replaced by the electrician.

Apprentices to silversmiths, sartors, and joiners were known as leather-apron boys. Helpers and underlings were called understrappers.

Once an important factor in the community, the ice-cutter who harvested precious ice from ponds, rivers, and lakes in cold weather, has been replaced by the electric refrigerator. The product of his efforts was preserved for hot weather by storing it, surrounded by thick layers of sawdust for insulation, in ice houses built in shady places with thick walls. Shiploads of ice were even sent to the tropics where, if any of the ice remained unmelted when it arrived,

A LACEMAKER

ICE CUTTERS

AN UMBRELLA MENDER

A WOODWOMAN

it commanded fabulous prices.

Changes among individuals with more responsible positions include the elimination of the stage-line agent and the packet-boat agent. The shopwalker in department stores has become a floor-walker, and the counter-jumper now has the more dignified title of salesman.

Little is heard these days of the union-buster who tried to discourage workers from joining a labor union or the strike-breaker who took the place of striking workers.

In addition, we seldom hear of the soldier of fortune, who would fight for any cause that promised profit, pleasure, and adventure, or the hireling and mercenary, who committed crimes or fought in wars merely for the pay involved.

The grave-robber and body-snatcher have just about disappeared, although

AN ORGAN GRINDER

A CHIFFONIER

CHAIRBEARERS AND LINKBOY

the cradle-snatcher, who marries very young girls, continues to bob up with a fair degree of frequency.

The Sharpener Men

Before almost everyone had an electric device for sharpening scissors, carving knives, and other cutting instruments, a common sight was the sharpener man with either a portable grindstone on his back or a wagon equipped with sharpening paraphernalia. In either case, he often had a brass bell that he rang incessantly as he traveled between jobs.

The housewife, hearing the bell, would gather up her dull scissors and knives and carry them to the curb, where the sharpener man worked on them. Being skilled at his work, he would give knives a sharpness they had never known before, and it was desirable to exercise some care in using a newly sharpened knife.

A SHARPENER MAN

5. The Servants

The Subjects

One of the great phenomena of our civilization has been the disappearance of the all-powerful oligarchs and, at the same time, the elimination of their underprivileged and oppressed subjects and lowly servants.

Thus, we have gotten rid of those at the top of our society and those at the bottom. They have been replaced, of course, by an upper class and a lower class, with a middle class in between, but the authority of the upper class has been greatly reduced and the lot of the lower class, though far from satisfactory, has been immeasurably improved.

Those men at the top were known as despots, tyrants, or autocrats if they were brutal and oppressive. If they were of "high birth" they were called nobles, patricians, silk stockings, bluebloods, or aristocrats. If their eminence was due to wealth, they were known as plutocrats.

Men of property, who usually were aristocrats, were called landed gentry, patroons, lords, masters, overlords, suzeraines, and squires.

Today we have no words describing owners of large tracts of land, except planter and plantation owner, and neither term necessarily connotes wealth or power. We have our magnates, moguls, and tycoons in the business world, but they have no counterparts in agriculture.

While the autocrats and despots were

disappearing, so were the people they ruled—their slaves and the cotters, hinds, peasants, peons, serfs, and villeins, who often were little more than slaves. Replacing them we have our paid farm-workers, sharecroppers, and tenant farmers, who may not have many luxuries but are free men and masters of their own destinies.

The Slaves

A slave was an unfortunate individual whose person and services were under the control of another; in other words, one who was owned by another person, did whatever he was told, and got no pay for doing it. In other countries, slaves often were taken as prisoners of war or purchased from pirates. Some were children purchased from their parents, and others were placed in slavery because they could not pay their debts. But in the United States, they were usually Negroes seized in the jungles of Africa and brought here in ships.

Slave-ship captains from New England often traded rum for a cargo of slaves, then sold them in the West Indies for a cargo of blackstrap molasses, which was carried to New England and used in making rum. After trading the molasses for rum, they set out again for Africa and repeated the process, making a nice profit each time on the three-way transaction, unless too many slaves died aboard ship before they could be sold.

In very early times, slaves or slaveys

AN ARISTOCRAT

SLAVE OWNERS

SLAVES IN THE COTTONFIELDS

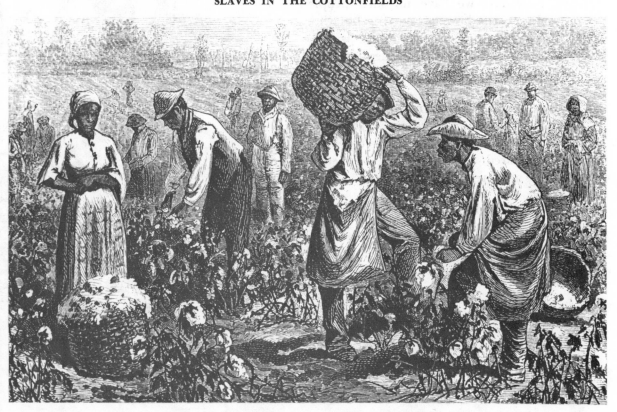

were called esnes, helots, and thralls; vassals and homagers were either slaves or lowly paid servants.

Bonds, bondmen, bondmaids, bond-women, and bondservants were slaves, either permanently or for a stated period, sometimes placed in servitude by parents who wanted to raise money or discharge indebtedness.

Persons desiring to come to the United States but lacking funds to pay for the passage bound themselves to be sold into service by the owner or master of a ship for a stated period, often up to seven and ten years. They were known as redemptioners or indentured servants. Thousands of such persons, including many skilled craftsmen, came here in that manner from Europe in the early days. Others became apprentices and learned a trade while indentured. They were forbidden to be married, incur debts, leave the vicinity, or take other employment until their indenture was terminated.

Nowadays we have no such people and the terms have left our vocabularies, except that we refer to "slave wages" when we mean low or inadequate pay.

When redemptioners became free from their obligations and when slaves were set free by their masters, they were called freemen or freedmen, freewomen or freedwomen. Those terms, too, have disappeared, because no one is a slave today and everyone is free.

The Slaveholders

The end of slavery also meant the disappearance of quite a few occupations, including the slaver or enslaver, who captured slaves in the jungle and threw them into servitude; the slaveship captain, who transported them to market; the slave trader, who sold them to their

A SLAVE DRIVER

owners for use in cultivating their plantations or for other purposes; and the frightful individual known as the slave driver, who dominated them in their work.

There were, of course, some slave drivers with a good measure of human kindness, but mention of the name usually brings to mind a cruel and heartless person with a long whip who exacted the last ounce of toil from every miserable slave, regardless of age, sex, or state of health.

The Menials

Being released from slavery was not always too great a boon, except spiritually, because a great many lowly, uneducated people worked in menial jobs in homes, taverns, and places of business for the smallest of wages. They often lived in misery approaching that which slaves had endured.

The human conscience, the labor unions, and the wage-hour laws have just about eliminated them: the cinderwenches, coistrells, creatures, drudges, ewers, fags, gillies, grubs, hackneys, peats, potboys, pot wallopers, rude boys, scrubs, scullery maids, scullions, and the like, who once existed at the bottom of our social order, often living on crumbs and slops, sleeping on boards or piles of straw in stables and cellars.

Even those unfortunates who cannot or will not work live a far better life today than the menial of a century or less ago, thanks to our charitable impulses.

SLAVES ON THE MARCH

The Household Servants

Until a few years ago, it was not uncommon to hear a housewife refer to her servants, meaning the individuals employed in her home. Today the term is in bad taste, except when applied to government officials who sometimes are mistakenly called public servants.

Among those formerly referred to as servants in larger domestic households were the abigail, lady's maid, lady's waiting maid, and lacewoman, who tended to milady's personal needs. There were the chambermaid and upstairs maid who took care of the bedrooms and upstairs sitting rooms. Downstairs were the cook, diningroom girl or waitress, pantrywoman, and parlor maid. In the basement, one found the washwoman, tubwoman, or laundress.

The large, formal establishment had its butler, footmen, valet, and chef, not to mention a gardener, coachman, and groom, plus perhaps a bootboy, useful man or assistant butler, chore man, and hall girl.

Nowadays, when a housewife is fortunate to have a dependable cleaning woman several days a week or a dayworker who does the ordinary household work by the hour, little mention is heard of upstairs maids and the like.

SELECTING A SERVANT

A LACEWOMAN

AN UPSTAIRS MAID

A BUTLER

A USEFUL MAN

A PANTRYWOMAN

A FOOTMAN

97

The Working Children

Before child labor came to be recognized as an evil, young boys and girls performed many functions in the social and business world, often working from dawn to bedtime, six or seven days a week.

Every commercial concern had an office boy, who also served as or was supplemented by an errand boy or runner, who delivered packages and carried messages. The office boy did odd cleaning jobs, such as a janitor does today, sharpened pencils, filled inkwells, wrapped packages, licked stamps, stuffed envelopes, and made himself generally useful. Big commercial establishments had cash boys, who took change to clerks who needed it and carried deposits to the bank.

In the business world, there also was the delivery boy, who delivered merchandise on foot, bicycle, or horse and wagon. Every construction gang had a waterboy or girl to fetch drinking water for the workers, and so did groups of farm workers out in the fields. Each church had a young organ pumper who kept the church organ going.

In larger homes, young boys and girls waited on tables, cleaned boots and shoes, cleaned and filled kerosene lamps, polished silver, and emptied slop jars. Others waved large fans to keep flies away from their employers. If their parents were employed in the household, the children usually received no pay of their own. At best, their wages were pitifully small.

Fishermen used boys on odd jobs, such as cleaning their catch, and the sailing vessels that carried passengers had a cabin boy to wait on the voyagers and run errands for the officers. The man-of-war and the fort, on land, both had boys called powder monkeys, who carried powder from the magazines to the guns, as needed. The man-of-war also had a loblolly boy who assisted the surgeon. Many of the street vendors were young-

AN OFFICE BOY

AN ERRAND BOY

A FISHBOY   A GILLIE BOY

CHILD SERVANTS

FEATHER WORKERS

101

sters, including the hot-corn girl and the muffin boy. Newsboys and newsgirls hawked newspapers on street corners in our larger cities. Young children did low-paid piecework at home, such as hemming handkerchiefs and stripping tobacco.

Feeble but laudable attempts to regulate child labor were made as early as 1904 in England, where a new law forbade custodians from permitting children to be in the streets or any public house to sing, play, perform, or sell be-tween the hours of 9:00 P.M. and 6:00 A.M.

Children between the ages of four and sixteen were forbidden to be in brothels, and children under sixteen could not be trained as acrobats or circus performers.

Thanks to Horatio Alger, Charles Dickens, and other observers, the practice of employing young children finally was outlawed by various child-labor laws, and today they are legally employed only in small family enterprises.

TOBACCO STRIPPERS

6. The Professionals

The Pedagogues

The person we now call a teacher or an instructor used to be known as a pedagogue or docent or else a master. There still are some masters today but they are teachers in private schools.

The instructor we now know as a dancing teacher was a dancing master. They also had fencing masters, drawing masters, music masters, singing masters, and schoolmasters, the latter being heads or principals of schools. Then there were women who instructed ladies in the arts of feather and quilt work, needlework, and embroidering.

Female teachers were called schoolmarms, if married or advanced in years, and schoolmistresses, if young and unmarried. Schoolmasters and schoolmarms used to correct bad deportment with a switch or ruler, or by assigning tasks such as cleaning blackboards and erasers, and penalized those pupils who failed to learn their lessons by putting them in a corner on a high stool, wearing a dunce cap.

The Preachers

Clergymen, reverends, pastors, and ministers were called by various other names in the olden days. The most common of them was preacher. The peripatetic preacher who traveled from town to town by carriage or on horseback was especially well-known.

Members of the clergy also were called parsons, predicants, dominies, and cassocks. Pulpiteer was a contemptuous term for a preacher, especially one who talked too much or too long. So was ranter.

A vicar was the name for a deputy or substitute preacher. The man who kept youngsters and dogs in order during the service, awakened nodding parishioners with a tithing stick, and made sure no one was loafing in the taverns during services was the tithing man.

The Scribes

Those who practice writing for an occupation have been called by many names, depending on the public estimate of their abilities, the era when they practiced, and their sex.

A female writer or literary woman

A MUSIC MASTER

A DRAWING MASTER

once was known as a bluestocking and later as a sob sister. The latter name was earned by those feminine newspaper reporters who used emotion to attract readers.

Names such as author and journalist are relatively new. Formerly such persons were known as penman, scribes, scrivers, and scriveners. Affectionately or familiarly, they sometimes were called quill pushers, inasmuch as they used quill pens in their work in the days before the typewriter and ballpoint pen.

Writers of inferior matter were called hacks, scrawlers, scribblers, and scribble-scrabbles.

The man who wrote in diary form was referred to as a diarist. If he wrote news, he was a gazeteer, gazette having been an early name for a newspaper. If a writer produced pamphlets, usually for political and propaganda purposes, he was a pamphleteer.

Some writers also gained recognition as pundits, expositors, and critics, but it was not necessary to write to earn those names.

The foregoing were writers of prose. Those who wrote ably in verse form—the poets of today—were referred to as scops, bards, or sonneteers, if they specialized in sonnets. However, if they wrote verses which had rhythm but did not quite qualify as poems, they were called rhymers, rimesters, versifiers, or poetasters.

A SCHOOLMISTRESS

A SCHOOLMASTER

106

A TITHINGMAN INSPECTS A TAVERN

A PULPITEER

A SCRIBE

The Barristers

A lawyer formerly was known by several other names which were imported from England and then sent back there. Among them were barrister, solicitor, and stuffgownsman, the latter being a junior barrister. Lawyers also were called shysters and pettifoggers if they used tricky or unethical methods.

Two other types of individuals, who often, but not necessarily, were lawyers, were the scrutator or scrutineer, who was an election judge, and the conveyancer, who transferred title to property and is now called a real-estate man. The surveyor was known as a boundary-goer or perambulator.

A physician once was known as a leech, because of the practice of using leeches to draw blood from patients. He also was called a sawbones, in recognition of his function as an amputator of limbs.

In the early days of this country, however, especially in the rural areas, the only individual available to act as physician and surgeon or chirurgeon was

A PETTIFOGGER

A SCRUTATOR

the local barber, who, in view of his experience in cutting hair and trimming beards, probably was a little better qualified than anyone else to assume the responsibility. The barber also performed as a dentist for purposes of tooth extraction, when no better trained specialist was available. The fact that the early barbers served also as surgeons is said to account for the red and white stripes found on all barber poles. The red stripe was an identification for those prospective patients who could not read.

Owing to the scarcity of trained physicians, medical fakers or peddlers of drugs had little difficulty in passing themselves off as doctors, thus facilitating the sale of their wares.

The veterinarian was known as a horse doctor; the former name is preferred by members of that profession because it covers more types of animals.

The Dragons

Until quite recently, young unmarried ladies in the so-called better circles never mingled socially with young boys except in the presence of a chaperone, known also as a dragon or duenna, whose duty it was to discourage and, indeed, prevent any hint of intimacy, no matter how harmless.

The chaperone usually was a mature, non-frivolous female of at least middle age and impeccable reputation. Grandmothers and unmarried aunts often were assigned to such service, on the assumption that they were strictly opposed to any kind of nonsense. They sat in or near the parlor when a young man came to call, moved to the kitchen if taffy was

ROE WHARTON EDWARDS

A DUENNA

to be pulled or corn popped, rode in the carriage when the young folks went for a ride, went along to socials and picnics if the young lady's parents were not to be present, and stood close by in the front hall while goodnights were being said.

Then the youngsters began going to the movies together, riding around in automobiles after dark, and doing a lot more dancing than they used to, with the result that the chaperone now is largely dispensed with.

We still hear of chaperones at large, formal gatherings, such as proms and balls, but they are little more than figureheads. The day of the working chaperone is past, except when groups of young, unmarried persons of both sexes are going to spend the night under one roof, as at a house party. And even then, modern chaperones are likely to be a recently-married young couple, who have others things on their minds than watching too closely over the morals of other young people.

Parents try to keep an eye on the young ones when it is possible to do so, but supervision has been sharply relaxed in most circles. Discriminating mothers reluctantly have come to accept the fact that it is all right for a young girl to be alone with a young man if he is known to the family and believed to be "the right sort." And mother does not worry when two or more couples are to be together. It is assumed that there is safety in numbers.

7. The Unusual People

The Dowsers

The "science" of dowsing or water-witching with a divining rod or doodle-bug is fading rather fast. Yet, there still are a few individuals who practice the "profession" in which, commonly, a forked stick is employed to locate the presence of water or minerals below the ground.

The divining rod, a V-shaped branch often taken from a witch hazel or willow tree, was held by the ends and moved about the area under inspection. The theory was that the joint would twist downward in the dowser's hands when held over a spot where water or minerals existed. Dowsers, known also as water-finders, water-smellers, and diviners, were employed to find a good spot to dig a well or a gold mine, and some built up a considerable reputation for accuracy, whether accidental or otherwise.

The *Encyclopaedia Britannica* states that the best dowsers have generally been more or less illiterate men, engaged in some humble vocation, and adds that the dowser's power lies beneath the level of conscious perception. It points out that dowsing dates back to the fifteenth century in Germany and that it has been the subject of much investigation.

The Scorchers

As the popularity of the bicycle grew, back in the eighties, a new problem arose. It involved the wheelman or cyclist, as the bicycle rider then was called, who operated his wheel at an excessive rate of speed, thus endangering pedestrians and other cyclists. The offender was referred to as a scorcher. Speed limits, ranging from five to ten miles an hour, had to be established, and scorchers who violated them were subject to being fined or jailed.

Bicycling in the latter part of the nineteenth century was a leading form of entertainment for both men and women. Special costumes were worn by the men and modest lady cyclists wore long, full skirts to conceal their limbs.

Occasional collisions occurred, as a result of careless riding, just as is the case with automobiles today. Long rides in the country were enjoyed by groups of cyclists, and bicycle racing was a popular form of sport.

Among the various types of cycles were those with one large wheel and one small one, and those which would carry from two to six persons.

A DOWSER

114

The Wagon Doctors

Another unusual individual was the wagon doctor, a charlatan who would buy up worn-out, broken-down wagons and restore them just enough to make them salable to unsuspecting persons who sometimes would not even get the newly acquired vehicle out to their farm before it collapsed. The wagon doctor moved from town to town and, naturally, was careful not to return to a community after he once had victimized the people there.

The duelist, a man who fought duels with pistols, swords, and other weapons when he decided that he or someone dear to him had been offended, was legislated out of existence, and even the hotheads have discontinued dueling in this country. The carpetbagger enjoyed a brief spell of notoriety after the Civil War and then faded out. The name was a term of contempt for a Northern opportunist who went South with his valise made out of carpeting to gain control of civil administration in the disorganized South and exploit the people.

The name also has been used for a man who stands for election in a district where he is a stranger, but was first

SCORCHERS

A SPIN THROUGH THE PARK

A FAMILY VEHICLE

applied in the Far West to a speculative banker who started in business with no assets other than those he could carry in a carpetbag and then absconded when he failed.

The end of the Civil War also marked the disappearance of the secessionist who wanted the South to withdraw from the Union and of the abolitionist who wanted to abolish slavery.

Long gone also is the barnstormer, a daredevil who used to thrill the public, especially in rural areas, with balloon ascensions and, later, airplane stunts, in the days when going up into space still was a great novelty. Every so often the barnstormer came to grief, thus adding to the thrill of the occasion.

The almoner or alms giver, who dispensed charity to the poor of behalf of others, usually benevolent and wealthy individuals, has largely been replaced by the Community Chest or some similar organization. With him have gone the poorhouse and the poor farm manager, whose function has been taken over by various welfare organizations and homes for the elderly and infirm. Recipients of private alms were called almsmen and almswomen.

BARNSTORMERS RISKING THEIR LIVES

The Hermits

We seldom hear today of a hermit or solitary, as he also was called, a man who preferred to live in seclusion—to live alone and be left alone. The hermit at one time lived in a hermitage for religious reasons, but in modern usage the name means one who lives alone because of a love for solitude or an aversion to society. A hermit generally resided in a hut or cave away from any town. He always was a ragged, unkempt individual and lived amidst filth and disorder. We have elderly people today

AN ALMONER

DUELISTS

A HERMIT

who want to be alone, but they are called recluses.

Children usually were afraid of hermits and avoided them, which was exactly what they wanted.

The Entertainers

Not even our transportation has changed more radically in the recent past than have our forms of entertainment. The clown survives in name, but uses new techniques. Formerly, he relied principally on his ludicrous actions and costumes to inspire his laughs. That was in the days when he was known as an antic, buffoon, droll, gracioso, harlequin, hobbyhorse, merry-andrew, mummer, pantaloon, punchinello, or zany. Only the court jester used wit as his chief stock in trade.

Nowadays, the clown, who usually is called a comedian or comic, entertains primarily via the spoken word and the gesture, with a few facial contortions thrown in. The circus clown still uses the old-time appeals but he is becoming scarcer each year.

The cinema threw the vaudevillian out of work and, while television brought him back, he returned as a performer on the air waves, rather than on the stage.

The movies and radio put an end to the old-time minstrel show, with its interlocutor and its hilarious endmen. The

A PUNCHINELLO

busker, who was a traveling actor, the troubador, the wandering minstrel, the itinerant jig dancer, the wandering fiddler, and the strolling ballad singer had disappeared even before the cinema came along.

The Foretellers

Today we have our forecasters, prognosticators, and opinion pollers who are respected for their ability to predict what will happen in the future because they rely on expert knowledge in making their predictions.

Back in the darker days, there were people who were believed to be able to foretell the future because of extraordinary intuition, communication with the dead, and so on. These individuals were known as augurs, clairvoyants, diviners, foretellers, foreboders, necromancers, presagers, seers and seeresses, soothsayers, and weirds.

The closest thing we have to such people today are the fortune teller, who uses a crystal ball, and the palmist or chiromancer, who relies on examination of the hand in making his predictions.

The Conjurers

When there were relatively more ignorant and superstitious people in the world than there are today, certain individuals were believed to have magical powers through connections with evil spirits. Among them were the conjurer or conjureman, the enchanter, the sorcerer and sorceress, the wizard, and the witch.

Witchcraft was a mighty unhealthy profession in colonial times. A witchwoman, commonly known as a witch, was supposed to be in league with the devil and to have the ability to throw spells over innocent victims. In Salem Village in Massachusetts, there was a wave of hysteria over witches in 1692, and hundreds of women were tried for the offense in four months. Nineteen are said to have been hanged, and one was pressed to death.

When we call someone a witch today, however, we do not mean to imply that she is practicing the "black art" or that she possesses supernatural power by compact with the devil. Rather we mean that she is either a crone or an old hag, or, conversely, that she is a charming or bewitching person.

No stigma attaches to another type of

A FORTUNE TELLER

person skilled in magic, the one known today as a magician, who entertains with sleight of hand. Formerly he was known also as a legerdemainist, prestidigitator, juggler, or hocus-pocus. The card player who uses sleight of hand in dealing or handling cards is not called a magician, but rather is referred to as a cardsharp.

A YOUNG WITCH ABOUT TO BE PUT IN STOCKS

AN OLD WITCH BEING OSTRACIZED

8. The Horse People

The Horse Riders

Until the automobile came into general use, the horse was the principal means of transporting individuals and goods from one place to another, so there were many occupations that centered on horse riding.

One was the delivery of mail and valuables, a job entrusted to the post rider and the express, who rode hard and fast from town to town to complete their missions. One especially well-known kind of horseman was the Pony Express rider.

The Pony Express was organized, just before the Civil War broke out, to carry mail, express, and valuables across the prairies and mountain states to the Far West. Fleet ponies, some five hundred of them, were used on the overland trail that ran from St. Joseph, Missouri, to Sacramento, California, a distance of 1,960 miles. So fast were the ponies and so rugged their riders that the trip was accomplished in ten days, by changing mounts and riders at frequent intervals. A competitive trip by stagecoach on a southern route required twenty-five days.

The express rider had to be a pretty tough and hardy individual and, in addition to being a talented horseman, had to be alert and resourceful, to protect himself against hostile Indians and hold-up men. There were eighty of these intrepid express riders.

The Pony Express route ran through Julesburg, Colorado; Scotts Bluff, Nebraska; Ft. Laramie and Casper, Wyoming; Salt Lake City, Utah; Carson City,

AN EXPRESS

A POST RIDER

CAVALRYMEN

Nevada; and Placerville, California. It ended at Sacramento because riverboats could take the mail from that city to San Francisco. However, the railroad, which could cover the distance much faster, soon took over from the express rider and made his job superfluous.

The cavalryman who rode a horse in battle, armed with a sword and carbine, was a vital part of our armed forces until jeeps, tanks, and other vehicles replaced the horse. The Rough Riders, as Teddy Roosevelt's cavalrymen were known at the time of the Spanish-American War, were famous for their furious charges and superb horsemanship.

Out in the cattle country, the buckaroo, as the cowboy or cowhand was called, relied on his trusty horse to carry him about the range, cut out steers from the herd, cope with stampedes, and fight off rustlers and Indians. Today, jeeps are coming to be widely used for the same work, minimizing the need for the horse trainer and the bronco buster.

Finally, there was the horsethief, the early predecessor of today's automobile thief. Hanging by the neck was considered the only proper punishment for a man who stole another man's horse.

The Animal Drivers

In the pulling of vehicles, horses shared the work with mules and oxen, and there also were pony carts, dog carts, donkey carts, and the like. Traffic jams involving vehicles pulled by animals were commonplace, just as they are today with motorized traffic. Yet not only the work animals, but also the many thousands of people who made a living driving those animals, have all vanished from the scene.

Gone in fact, though not in name, is the teamster, the man who once drove the two, four, eight, or more horses that pulled freight of all kinds from wharf or depot to factory and warehouse, from warehouse to retail store, and from town to town.

The fact that today's truck driver, who has replaced the teamster or waggoner, belongs to the International Brotherhood of Teamsters, Chauffeurs, Warehousemen and Helpers Union, known as the Teamster's Union, does not make him a teamster, nor does he so call himself. The truck driver is just

A BUCKAROO

A TEAMSTER

FIRE-ENGINE DRIVERS

GOING TO A FIRE IN NEW YORK CITY

as hardy and vociferous, just as rough and ready, as any teamster ever was, but he is not a teamster.

Also displaced by the truck driver are the muleteer or mule skinner, who drove mule teams; the bull-wagon boss; the bullwacker; the oxman; and the ox-train master; not to mention the drayman, who drove a dray; the carter or cartman, who drove a cart which was a two-wheeled wagon; and the omnibus driver, an omnibus having been a small horse-drawn bus used for intracity transportation.

We no longer have the hackman or jarvey, who drove the hack, and the horsecar driver who preceded the motorman on the street car.

Hordes of delivery wagons crowded the streets of every town of any size. There were drivers of wagons delivering ice, groceries, meat, fish, fruits and vegetables, coal, lumber, feed, bakery goods, and so on, plus the drivers of horse-drawn sprinkler wagons, hearses, and ambulances, including horse ambulances. In cold weather, many of these same drivers shifted to sleds and sleighs.

One unique horse driver was the tobacco roller, who used a team of horses or oxen to roll huge hogsheads of tobacco from farm to wharf. Another was the packhorse driver, usually mounted on another horse himself, who used a horse or mule as a light truck on prospecting expeditions. Still another was the charioteer, who, in early colonial times, drove a small two-wheeled passenger vehicle resembling a Roman chariot.

The Horse Handlers

Horse riders and drivers were not the only ones to lose out when the work horse and the carriage horse began to vanish from the scene. Horse handlers, drafthorse breakers, horse trainers, and nagsmen all found themselves dispensable.

The horse trader or chanter, known as a deceitful and slippery individual, who would cheat his own mother-in-law, was another casualty, as was the knacker, who operated a horse ambulance and dealt in old and expired horses.

The barn boss and barnhand found themselves looking for other work as large concerns replaced their work

A MISHAP WITH A DONKEY CAR

**A DRAYMAN WITH A
RUNAWAY TEAM**

**AN OMNIBUS DRIVER
WITH A FULL LOAD**

A BANDWAGON DRIVER

A HORSETRAIN DRIVER

A HITCH-STABLE OWNER

horses with trucks. The liveryman or hitch stable owner gradually lost his tenants and his customers. His employees, the currier, the hostler or ostler, and the horse baiter or feeder, also became unemployed.

The farrier, now known as a horse-shoer, stayed in business only if he cared to confine himself to shoeing saddle horses for riding academies, race tracks, and country gentlemen.

The impact on the community, following the disappearance of the horse, was as severe as if we were suddenly to stop using automobiles and trucks, and all the chauffeurs, garages, filling stations, and automobile agencies were to be forced out of business.

The Coachmen

There were two types of coaches: the stagecoach, which corresponded to the

A COACH OWNER

A HORSE TRAI

intercity bus of today, and the private coach, which served the same purpose as a limousine or sedan.

The stagecoach carried passengers on a regular route from town to town and back again, pausing at inns and taverns along the way for meals and to discharge and pick up passengers, and stopping overnight, if the trip were long enough. The crew typically consisted of a stagecoach driver and sometimes a rifleman, also called a shotgun, who acted as a guard. The stagecoach usually was pulled by four or six horses that were changed in relays, if the route was a long one.

The private coach often was a more

A STAGECOACH DRIVER

A MAIL-WAGON DRIVER

elaborate and comfortable vehicle, driven by a liveried coachman, or whip, who had beside him an assistant known as a man-on-the-box, who served as a relief reinsman and as a footman to open the doors for passengers, help them in and out of the coach, load luggage, and so on.

When necessary, a postillion rode on the back of one of the coach horses to serve as a guide, and there might be one or more outriders or outrunners for protection from brigands or other highwaymen. When traveling on a dark night in strange territory, the well-appointed coach had at least one linkman or linkboy who carried a torch out front to light the way. Any of these individuals might also act as a harbinger, forerunner, or precursor, who ran ahead and arranged for lodgings at an inn or tavern or perhaps a private estate.

The veteran coachman took great pride in his four-in-hand outfit, known also as a coach-and-four or coach-and-six, depending on the number of horses being used.

The arrival of a coach at a tavern was the occasion for much scurrying around, especially if the passengers and horses

AN OXTRAIN MASTER

A TOBACCO ROLLER

136

A SLEIGH DRIVER

were to remain overnight. In that case, the hostlers would care for the horses, and the porters and flunkies would attend to the baggage, while the host would serve drink and food in the taproom and assign beds to the patrons.

The Carriagemakers

Every town of any size had one or more establishments for the manufacture and repair of coaches, carriages, wagons, and wheels, often known as the wagon works or carriage works. Thus, there were such self-explanatory jobs as:

coachmaker	wagon master
coachmonger	wagonmonger
waggoner	wagonsmith
waggonfiller	wagonwright
wagongreaser	wheelsmith
wagonman	wheelwright
	wainwright

Carriages alone accounted for numerous jobs, such as:

carriage builder	carriage maker
carriage cleaner	carriage monger
carriage driver	carriage painter
carriage ironer	carriage springer
carriage joiner	carriage trimmer
carriage lampman	carriage worker

When we add to all these employed people such others as the hay, grain, and feed store owner, the makers of horse blankets, horse troughs, hitching posts, horse or carriage blocks, and the harness maker, it is not hard to visualize the great change that came over the community when the horse age began to approach its end.

COACHES IN THE SNOW

9. The Transportation People

The Mariners

The passing of the sailing ship meant the disappearance, too, of the shipmaster or packetship master and the cabin boy or shipboy. It also marked the end of the foretopman, the foremastman, and other crewmen, known also as jack tars, old salts, mariners, searovers, shipmen, seafarers, shellbacks, and seadogs, who raised and lowered the sails in foul weather and good.

Then the gradual passing of the coal-fired steamship saw, in turn, the disappearance of the coal passer, who helped load coal on the boat, and the stoker who endured terrific heat down in the hold, keeping the engines supplied with fuel.

Gone, too is the harpooner, who harpooned whales by hand in the old days.

The Shipbuilders

In the days when sailing ships and men-of-war were made of boards and planks, the ship builder was known as a shipwright or boatwright.

He was dependent for help on such other local businessmen as the master ropemaker, roper, or staymaker, who fashioned the maze of ropes needed to operate the vessel (another worker with the latter title made stays for ladies' corsets), the ship joiner who did the fancy woodwork, the mastmaker who

A HARPOONER

AN OLD SALT IN A GALE

140

made the lofty wooden masts, the calker or caulker, who sealed the joints between the planks in the sides, deck, and bottom of the vessel, and the sailmaker who made the canvas sails.

Related workers were the figurehead maker or carver, if he were really talented, who carved the figurehead—either a beast or human figure—found on the prow of every sailing ship worthy of the name, and the provisioner or ship's chandler, who provided the food, supplies, and equipment needed by an ocean-going ship.

The Boatmen

A great upheaval in occupations followed the coming of the railroad, steamship, and automotive vehicle. Each caused the elimination of a group of jobs that once seemed as enduring as the oak.

The spread of the railroads meant a quick end to the rapid expansion of the network of canals in the Eastern and Middlewestern States. Some five thousand miles of canals, with their locks, tollhouses, tollgates, and taverns, had been built or started when the iron horse came along in the late 1820's and gradually began to offer faster and cheaper transportation of passengers and freight.

Although a few important canals have remained in service, for the hauling of freight alone, millions of dollars of supposedly blue-chip investments were destroyed in a short time as the railroads paralleled the canals and took over their cargoes.

The end of canal travel in all but a few places meant the rapid disappearance of such occupations as towpath driver, canaller, hoggie, canalboatman, steersman, lockhand, tolltaker, and toll-

MARINERS REEFING A SAIL

SAILMAKERS

STOKERS

house keeper, plus the boat puffer, whose job it was to praise his employer's boat and spread false rumors about competitive boats wherever prospective ticket buyers gathered.

Adaptation of the steam engine to the riverboat meant the elimination of the keelboatman and the sweepsman and poleman, who propelled river craft of various kinds. It signalled the end, too, of the bateauman or flatboatman, whose boat also was known as an ark and broadhorn.

The riverway peddler or storeboatman began to vanish when the first trucks appeared. While they remained in business, the operators of these trade boats would blow a horn or trumpet as the boats were about to stop at a landing, so as to announce the arrival and attract customers.

The era of high-speed travel has also brought about a rapid reduction in the number of ferryboats as costly bridges and tunnels are built to save time, thus causing the elimination of the ferryboat captain and the ferryman.

The Trolleymen

Less than a quarter of a century ago, the street car or trolley car that ran down the main streets of all our larger cities and towns, traveling on rails and propelled by electricity taken from an overhead wire or underground cable, seemed as permanent as the carbarn. But today the street car is gone from all but a handful of cities because the bus, powered by gasoline or diesel oil,

has proved to be more flexible and more economical to operate. Disappearing along with the street car are the motorman and conductor, once solid figures in our urban society, and their war-time counterparts, the motorwoman and conductorette.

The motorman drove the trolley car and kept the track clear to the best of his ability by clanging repeatedly on a loud bell with a foot pedal, when a horse and wagon got in front of the car. The

COAL PASSERS

A FIGUREHEAD

SHIPWRIGHTS

A STEERSMAN

SWEEPSMEN

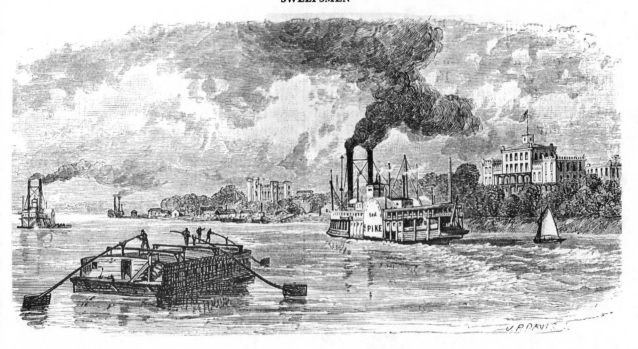

TWO CANALLERS

A LOCKHAND

146

motorman's function still is performed on subway trains but there he is called an engineer.

The conductor was the man who rode in back to take the fares and ring them up on a visible register, help women—especially young and pretty ones—on and off the car, call out the streets and stops, and chase away young boys who tried to hitch free rides. He also used to put the trolley back on the wire when it came off and reversed its direction when the car reached the end of the line and was ready to start back.

Actually the conductor faded out first, because economy-minded management discovered that the motorman could take fares as well as guide the car, and also call out the streets if he cared to. Under this system, the conductor's function of helping customers on and off the car was just quietly abandoned. In place of the motorman and conductor we have the bus driver. The trolleyman who serviced and repaired the trolley cars has been replaced by a garage mechanic.

A MOTORMAN

TROLLEYTRACK LAYERS

The Railroaders

The railroads are still very much with us, as are their crews, consisting of engineer, fireman, conductor, brakeman, trainman, and the like, but two of those jobs remain in name only.

The change from coal to diesel oil on all railroads, except those where electricity is used, has relieved the fireman of the job of throwing wood or shovelling coal into the firebox of the locomotive and taking on water from the tall tanks located alongside the tracks. Instead he now checks the operation of the diesel engines, turns valves when oil is taken on, and is a sort of assistant engineer. But like the teamster, he retains his traditional name.

The general adoption of airbrakes also has changed the duties of the brakeman, who now has to set brakes by hand only in an unusual emergency. He spends his time nowadays calling out stations, setting out flares when the train stops unexpectedly between stations, opening doors to passenger coaches when the train stops in a station, assisting ladies with their baggage, helping old people and children on and off the train, and performing other jobs having nothing to do with brakes. The handcar, once pumped by hand, now is completely motorized.

A BRAKEMAN

HANDCAR PUMPERS

149

TRAIN ROBBERS

Gone physically as well as in name is the crossing guard, who used to lower the gates when a train approached at grade level, sometimes holding out a sign that said "Stop," to warn pedestrians that it was dangerous to cross. He has been replaced by all sorts of automatic electric devices, not to mention overpasses and underpasses that make accidents impossible.

10. The Farm Folk

The Milkmaids

Everyone who has driven across the country in recent years knows that the farm has felt the full effects of the machine age. Most functions formerly done by hand are now being done more quickly and less expensively by machine, and many operations once carried out in at least a small way on every farm now are being performed on a large scale on fewer farms.

On many modern farms one no longer finds the cow shed, the chickenhouse, the pigpen, the orchard, or the vegetable garden. Farmers are becoming specialists, producing their specialty for sale and buying their everyday needs in town.

The milking machine has largely replaced the milkmaid and the dairymaid who used to help milk the cows and handle the milk on the family farm. The plowman and plowboy also have disappeared, no longer needed to drive the horse or mule and guide the plow along the furrow. That work, like much other work on the farm, has been taken over by a tractor driver who would not know which end of a mule to hitch a plow to.

A MILKMAID

The Flailers

Becoming scarcer also are the sower, who used to plant seeds by hand, the corn picker, who used to pick corn by hand, the corn husker, who stripped the leaves from the ear, and the corn shocker, who piled the corn stalks into tall shocks. There are machines that do the whole job today.

The cradler, mower or reaper, who used to cut the grain with a scythe and cradle and the flailer, who threshed it with a wooden flail, are long since gone.

Following them are the gleaner, who picked up cut grain by hand, the wheat shocker, who used to pick up the bundles of grain dropped by the binder and arrange them in shocks, and the wheat shock pitcher, who fed the bundles of grain into the threshing machine or separator, and the thresherman who operated the machine. They have been replaced by another machine that cuts, threshes, and bags the grain all in one operation, leaving the straw on the ground to be raked up and baled by still another machine.

The hay maker, hay loader, hay

CORN HUSKERS

HIRED HANDS

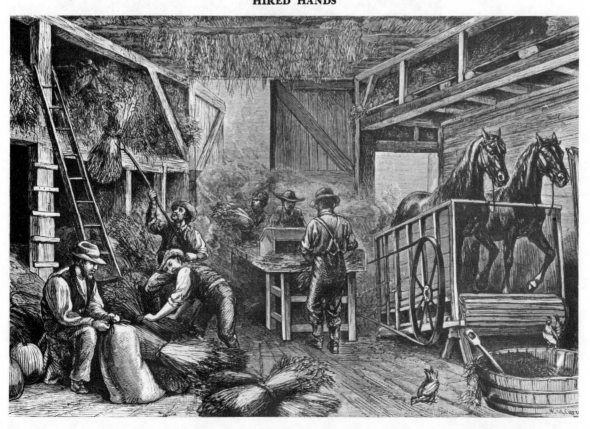

pitcher, and hay wagon driver, who used to harvest the hay; the tedder, who turned the hay over in the field to facilitate drying, and the hay presser, who baled it, are fast being replaced by an ingenious machine that does the entire job of getting in the hay. The haystack has become a curiosity, and the skilled haystacker is almost impossible to find.

The Hired Men

The hired man—that faithful man of all work—who used to toil from dawn to dusk or later at a wide variety of chores also is vanishing, along with most of the chores he used to perform. Each year there are fewer farms with horses to be brought in from the field and then

FLAILERS

fed, curried, and harnessed up, fewer cows to be milked, fewer pigs to be fed, fewer chickens to be cared for, while machines do much of the other work that used to keep him so busy. When non-family labor is needed at harvest time, the farmer hires workers from town by the day or hour, at wage rates which would sound mighty attractive to the old-time hired hand who worked for room, board, and a modest monthly wage.

With the disappearance of the hog from so many farms, the voice of the hog caller is being stilled. Out in the country, we no longer hear of the drover, or cowherd or neatherd, who used to drive herds of cattle along the trail, nor do we meet the shepherdess or the swanherd, the goosegirl, or the goose picker. Rail splitters, too, are gone, now that fences are made of boards and posts and wire.

Missing from the farm scene, also, are the fodderer or fogger, who used to feed the cattle, the crop watcher with his shotgun, as well as that non-human farm hand, the scarecrow, that once used to frighten crows and other birds away from the garden and the corn patch. The limeburner and charcoal maker, who usually were farmers, have all but vanished, as has the bee hunter, who trailed bees to their hive and then appropriated their honey. And we never see the bridge owner, a farmer who used to build a bridge—often a covered bridge—over a stream that ran through his property and then charge a toll for its use by others.

A HAYRAKER

11. The Descriptive Appellations

The Favorable Names

So far we have been dealing with names applied to people who were engaged in various occupations, but there also is a long list of interesting names or appellations we have applied to individuals who have had certain pronounced characteristics, habits, shortcomings, or other attributes which usually are not occupations and yet help to classify the person and describe his place in our society.

To explain the distinction, when we say that a man is a barber, we describe his occupation. If we also say that he is an inebriate, we describe a significant characteristic which is in no sense an occupation, not even an avocation, although some people work at it rather consistently.

Saying that a man is a lawyer tells us how he makes his living; adding that he is a miser tells us what sort of person he is.

There are, of course, some borderline cases. One whom we call a swindler or burglar probably does not devote his entire attention to swindling or burglary. He may be a swindler by night but a salesman in the daytime. He may burgle only now and then and devote himself to some more legitimate enterprise the rest of the time.

In analyzing these descriptive appellations, many of which are seldom or never heard these days, we find that they fall into two groups—those which are favorable and those which are unfavorable, known also as epithets. The first group is much easier to dispose of.

Well-mannered, intelligent people too often are taken for granted, because

CRONIES

BOONFELLOWS

157

NOBS

good deportment attracts far less attention than misbehavior. In addition, there are many more ways to be bad than to be good. Hence, although we have scores of names for unfortunate or bad-mannered people, there are relatively few descriptive names for respectable individuals and, for some reason, we fail to make full use of the modest assortment of appellations that is available.

For example, in referring to a close friend today we often call him a pal or chum or buddy, using those same words over and over. Yet there is no reason why we should not recall from the past such descriptive substitutes as boonfellow, playfellow, or yokefellow. We also can use billy, comate, copemate, crony, eme, fere, frater, or make. Thus, we would have fourteen ways of refer-

A DUDE

ring to a pal instead of a mere three.

A gay companion can be called a Trojan, and a lively friend a birkie, caperer, cavorter, frolicker, larker, grig, merrymaker, reveller, or rollicker. However, if the latter is boisterous, he becomes a romp or skylarker, which are not favorable.

In talking about a girl of good reputation, instead of always calling her a skirt or dame, we can refer to her as a duck, duckling, filly, heifer, or kitty. Other possibilities are burd, chit, cummer, dawtie, dowsabel, lass, or snab. If she is a gentle soul, one can call her a kitten or lamb, and if she is graceful, a swan. If she is half fish, she is a mermaid. A quiet girl can be referred to as a mouse. A feminine singer can be a canary, chantress, songbird, thrush, or warbler.

There even are some nice alternate names for a young boy if he is well-behaved, including: calf, callant, colt, gossoon, kid, sapling, slip, spadger, sprig,

A DANDY

sprout, shaver, shaveling, or stripling.

A small child is a bairn, balding, cherub, chick, chickabiddy, moppet, pee-wee, tad, toddler, tot, trot, or tyke. A first child is a firstling, and an infant is a bantling or nestling. A youngster of either sex can be called a chicken, youngling, or younker.

The head of the house, if a man, is a goodman, and his wife is a goodwife unless she is of lowly station, in which case she becomes a goody.

A clever, superior, outstanding man, whom we tend to call a humdinger or hot-shot, can be called a crackajack, marvel, magnifico, non-pareil, prodigy, pip, pippin, ripper, stemwinder, shark, topper, tops, trump, outstander, whale, or wizard.

A proficient person is an adept or past master, an expert is a dab, an honest man is a truepenny. A person of charm is a spellbinder or enthraller, a pure person is a dove, and a champion is a paladin. A wise man is a Nestor, owl, sage, Solomon, or solon, while one of superior position is a nob, hence the Nob Hill section of San Francisco, where all the swells lived.

A strong man is a buck, husky, ironside, moose, ox, or snoozer, a man of great fortitude is a Spartan or stalwart, a sturdy man is a horse, and a tenacious chap is a bulldog. A person of spirit is a sparkplug or ball of fire, and a brave man is a lion.

The Unfavorable Names

The world must always have been supplied with objectionable, vicious, unlawful, and immoral people, judging by the array of names that has been developed for referring to such persons. While some of these names are archaic or obsolete, and many came from foreign lands, they once were in common use and are available today to lend color to our everyday conversations.

Back when forms of entertainment were far fewer, people had much more time to observe and think about each other—critically and otherwise. Much of the time now spent listening to the radio, watching television, attending the movies, witnessing sports events, and riding about in automobiles formerly was devoted to idle gossip. Comment about the more unusual members of the community—the non-conformers and unfortunates—helped to pass the time when nothing more interesting was taking place. Instead of being an object of pity, the unfortunate individual too often

was a source of entertainment for the idle, the infirm, and the aged, a kind of sideshow that brightened up their drab lives.

Thus, fifty and a hundred years ago the miser, the spendthrift, the loafer, the drunk, the braggart, the blunderer, the hag, the thief, the bully, the simpleton, and other out-of-the-ordinary people received far more attention than they do today, when there are so many other objects of interest. Talking about them and developing new names for them was one way of avoiding boredom.

The Dudes

As recently as the early 1900's when the ratio of city residents to country dwellers was much lower than it is now, the person dressed in city attire was rather conspicuous if he visited rural and backwoods areas where clothing was coarse and crude. Even if he was not overdressed by city standards, he attracted attention and unfavorable comment.

As a term of ridicule, mingled perhaps with envy, the rustics and frontiersmen applied the name dude to anyone dressed up like a city fellow, and back in the city the term came to designate anyone who was overly solicitous about his attire and preoccupied with style and personal adornment.

Today there are so many well-dressed people in the cities, and country people dress so much better than they used to, that a man with a collar and tie, a jacket, creases in his pants, and a watch on his wrist no longer stands out the way he formerly did, not even if he wears a homburg and a fancy waistcoat. Indeed, styles have evolved in such a way that it is difficult for a man to appear overdressed these days. The result is that we seldom hear talk about dudes, and, indeed, we have no modern substitute for the term, unless it be clotheshorse or fashion plate, both of which miss the mark.

The word dude still endures in the term dude ranch, but in that connection carries no hint of ridicule. A dude ranch merely is a place where well-heeled city folk go to enjoy outdoor life and horse riding.

The Fops

Although a dude sometimes is called a fop or dandy, those names usually refer to someone even more fastidious about his dress and more extreme in his attire.

Other names for fops, used principally in Europe, are: barbermonger, Beau Brummel, buck, exquisite, fancy man, jackadandy, macaroni, puppy, spangle baby, spark, swell, and toff.

Beau Brummel, who was a fashion authority and dandy in England back in the days of George IV, was the leader of a cult consisting of a band of young men "whose insolent and affected manner made them universally unpopular," according to one observer. A typical costume for these dandies consisted of a coat of blue or brown cloth with brass buttons and coat tails almost touching their heels, very tight breeches of buckskin, highly polished Hessian boots, a waistcoat buttoned incredibly tight to produce a small waist and opening at the breast to exhibit a frilled shirt and cravat.

Members of London's Macaroni Club, on the other hand, dressed in white silk breeches, very tight coats and vests, enormous white neckcloths, white silk stocks, and red heeled shoes with diamond buckles.

The Hayseeds

The opposite of a dude was a hayseed, one of the many uncomplimentary names that city people applied to rural residents, most of whom were plainly and often crudely dressed in their skins and homespun or overalls. It was customary to picture them with pointed beards, hay sticking from their long hair, and wearing muddy boots or going barefoot. It also was commonly believed, or alleged, that country people as a class were crude, ignorant, unsophisticated, awkward, and ludicrous to behold even when dressed in their best. This accounts for some of the names unfairly applied to them.

The most common of those names were hick, hayseed, and yokel, but farmers and rural workers also were called jakes, jaspers, rubes, and reubens after given names that were fairly common in the early days.

Other names for a hayseed were appleknocker, bogtrotter, bucolic, chawbacon, cidersqueezer, clodhopper, bumpkin, hob, hobbinol, hobnail, homespun, joskin, rustic, sodbuster, tyke and yap.

The Misfits

Back when many people had little education or social training, it was only natural that there were many misfits and unfortunates and many names for such people.

Those who were afflicted with manual clumsiness were known as bobblers, bogglers, dubs, duffers, fumblers, and tinkers. Persons who were merely awkward and clumsy were called galoots, gawks, gawkies, hobbledehoys, lobcocks, lobsters, loobies, louts, lubbers, lummoxes, oafs, puts, schlemiels, slobs, stiffs, and swabs.

If an adult was ragged and unclean, he was a ragamuffin, slorp, sloven, slubberdegullion, or tatterdemalion, while if a youngster or youth was dirty and ragged, and probably delinquent as well, he was referred to as a gamin, guttersnipe, mudlark, or street arab.

A mangy person was a ronyon, and a lazy one was a slouch; hence, the ex-

A TOSSPOT

pression, "He's no slouch," meaning he is an able or active person.

An individual who was a bit queer—off his trolley, a screwball, or nut—was known as a bird, cove, cuckoo, cuss, queer fish, gazabo, gink, or oddball.

Another type of misfit is the person who uses alcohol to excess—the alcoholic or drunk as we call him. Among the names applied to this unfortunate through the years are: bacchant, barfly, bibber or winebibber, boozer, carouser, debaucher, fuddler, inebriate, lush, rumhound, rummy, rumpot, soak, sot, souse, stumblebum, tippler, toper and tosspot.

On the other hand, anyone who refrained completely from the use of alcoholic beverages—a dry—was known as a teetotaler or abstainer. Teetotalers were greatly in the minority in colonial days when the water supply often was suspect and almost everyone relied on homemade beer, ale, cider, or wine as everyday beverages.

A SOUSE

The Ignoramuses

Before we had compulsory education and such educational media as television and the movie palace, there were a great many ignorant, stupid, and mentally deficient folk and almost as many names for describing them. We tend to overuse terms such as goof, fool, and idiot, although there are scores of alternatives to draw on, including an imposing group that end in -head, -pate, -brain, -poll, and -skull, presumably because the head is the seat of knowledge. Among them are:

beetlehead	heavyhead
blockhead	hoddypeak
blunderhead	hoddypoll
bonehead	loggerhead
bubblehead	lughead
bullhead	lunkhead
buttonhead	knucklehead
clogpate	meathead
clogpoll	muddlehead
chowderhead	muttonhead
chucklehead	noddypoll
doddypoll	pinhead
dumbhead	rattlebrain
dunderhead	rattlehead
dunderpate	rattlepate
emptyhead	rattleskull
fathead	saphead
featherbrain	scatterbrain
featherhead	sheepshead
fiddlehead	softhead
hammerhead	thickhead
woodenhead	

Then there is a long list of names from the animal world that have been applied to ignorant and stupid people, including names of birds and fish:

ass	gowk
coot	jackass
cuddy	jay
daw	moke
dodo	mutt
donkey	smelt
gander	swine
goose	widgeon
gosling	woodcock

In addition, anyone seeking variety in referring to such people has a choice of these names:

boob	lurdan
booby	moron
changeling	mooncalf
chump	motley
coof	natural
cudden	niddering
cuif	nincompoop
dizzard	ninny
dolt	ninnyhammer
dromedary	nitwit
dunce	noddy
dullard	noodle
dumbbell	patch
dummy	sap
foozle	silly
gaby	simp
gomeral	simple
gump	simpleton
halfwit	soft
hash	stock
haversel	stupid
hobbil	sumph
hoddydoddy	totty
idiot	tomfool
ignoramus	wampus
juggins	witling
lob	zany
lug	

The Loafers

In Colonial times, loafing was a serious offense, much more so than it is today. Anyone seen spending too much time standing around doing nothing or lingering too long in a public drinking place or anyone refusing to work was referred to as an idler and was subject to fine and imprisonment.

Fines were assessed against those who tarried longer than an hour, sometimes a half hour, in a tavern during working hours. With so many people who had nothing to do except watch out for idlers there was little chance of getting away with anything.

The idler also was known as a bum, bummer, do-nothing, drone, faitour, lollard, lounger, pool hall loafer, slounger, sloth, sluggard, or village loafer. If he was a bit off his rocker as well as an idler, he was called the town character.

DO-NOTHINGS

IDLERS

The Filchers

The thief, robber, and burglar, as we call those who illegally take things that belong to another, always have been held in low esteem. They formerly were called by such names as crib, filcher, fingerer, ladrone, larcener, lifter, lurcher, picklock, pilferer, pincher, purloiner, rook, scrounger, shark, sharper, scourer, sneak thief, snatcher, taker, thimblerig, yegg, or yeggman.

Bandits were known as brigands, larceners, marauders, outlaws, riflers, swagmen, and waylayers, while the highjacker, who now confines himself pretty much to holding up trucks and warehouses, was called a highwayman, gentleman-of-the-road, bushranger, and road agent. The cudgeler or cudgleboy now is referred to as a hoodlum.

The modern mugger, hold-up man, purse snatcher, and gunman have replaced the cutthroat, cutpurse, footman, footpad, hornthumb, nightwalker, pad, ripper, and sandbagger. The invention of the revolver, which is a more reliable weapon than the sandbag, though noisier if discharged, undoubtedly inspired some of the changes in tactics among these offenders and hence some of the name changes.

The Pirates

Pirates who used to seize ships, together with their cargoes, passengers, and crews, were quite numerous back when nations were at war more often than not—in the days of the Spanish Main. In fact, it often was difficult to draw the line between acts of piracy and legitimate naval action when ship captains carried letters of marque in which their monarchs authorized them to make a prize of the enemy's ships and merchandise.

Much depended on your personal point of view. A pirate who captured an enemy vessel and brought it back to home port loaded with treasure was, of course, a local hero, not a law-breaker, to his fellow countrymen.

Piracy was carried on in the Mediterranean Sea in the days of the Roman Empire and later was practiced on a broad scale by the Barbary pirates or Moors from Algeria and Tunis. Then it mushroomed in the West Indies and off

LOLLARDS

POOLROOM LOAFERS

HIGHWAYMEN

GENTLEMEN OF THE ROAD

FOOTMEN RECONNOITERING

the coast of the Carolinas, where pirates found it relatively easy to hide when pursued.

A typical pirate has been described as "a sea-faring man who detests steady work with its small rewards and prefers a life of danger with a prospect of acquiring sudden wealth."

When a man joined a pirate crew, there were no questions asked and no wages paid, except that every crew member received an agreed-on share of any profits that might accrue. Ships that started out with letters of marque in time of war oftimes turned to piracy if their legitimate mission did not pay well enough.

Some pirates are said to have started in business by stealing a small boat with which they boarded and captured a

A PILFERER CAUGHT IN THE ACT

larger sailing vessel, taking it by surprise under cover of darkness. Then with the larger boat they captured a still larger one and so on until they obtained a craft that was fast enough and armed well enough to serve their purpose.

With radio and seaplanes available to hunt down law-breakers, it is unlikely that there will be any widespread revival of piracy, but it was big business in the day of the sailing vessel, when it was relatively easy to elude and hide from pursuers.

Pirates were variously known as buccaneers, corsairs, freebooters, picaroons,

BUCCANEERS

A DECOY

A SHARPER

A TRAVELING MOUNTEBANK

privateers, rovers, seadogs, and sea wolves. Although criminals by today's standards, in most cases, their numbers included many colorful figures.

Among the more famous pirates were Edward Teach, known as Blackbeard, who was killed in 1718 and two women, Anne Bonny and Mary Read. The *Encyclopaedia Britannica* states that another pirate—Captain Kidd—was no pirate at all, having been a scapegoat for others. In the absence of pirates, the high seas are safer but at the same time less interesting.

The pillager, who looted communities instead of seizing ships, also was called a despoiler, forager, forayer, plunderer, rapparee, ravager, reaver, or sacker. He, too, is a man of the past.

The Hornswogglers

Back when the general public was much more gullible than it is today, swindlers and deceivers were even more numerous, relatively, than they now are, and there were many names for them, including: bilker, blackleg, boodler, bamboozler, cozener, defalcator, flim-flammer, finagler, fainaiguer, gam-

A FLIMFLAMMER

moner, grifter, gyp, gentleman-of-fortune, hawk, hoodwinker, hornswoggler, jackleg, nobbler, over-reacher, shark, sharpie, sharper, sharpshooter, skin, slicker, snap, short-changer, trickster, and wimpler.

A person who was easily taken in by a swindler—a sucker, dupe, or fall guy, as we call him today—was known as a chouse, cull, cully, dotterel, geck, gudgeon, gull, mug, or pigeon.

Then, the come-on man for a gambler or swindler—the one who locates the sucker and leads him in for the kill—was a barnard, buncosteerer, capper, decoy, or shill, while a race-track tout was a steerer, tipster, or touter.

The No-Good Persons

Through the years there have been several types of no-good persons, usually males. The individual we often refer to as a scamp or rascal also used to be called a hempseed, kite, knave, limmer, loon, lown, miscreant, picaro, rapscallion, scalawag, scapegrace, or spalpeen.

A wandering rascal or vagrant, who was one step lower than a tramp, was called a caird, gangrel, landlouper, mounteback, rogue, skellum, snoozer, sundowner, vagabond, waff, or waffie. A fugitive from justice or from trouble—a runaway—was a runagate or skedaddler.

RUNAGATES

A SNIPJACK

A SCALAWAG CAUGHT WITH THE EVIDENCE

A scoundrel was a bezonian, black-guard, reprobate, or varlet. A mean, worthless, low-down despicable scoundrel, on the other hand, commonly called a wretch or jerk, formerly was known by such names from the lower forms of animal life as:

buzzard	mongrel
creature	rat
cur	rodent
dog	skunk
earthworm	slug
hound	snake
lapdog	snipe
louse	varmint
messan	vermin
	worm

Other names for worthless persons were:

bugger	off-scouring
caitiff	rotter
crumb	scab
cullion	scum
gallows bird	scut
hilding	snipjack
losel	snot
naught	sow-gelder
	whoreson

A group of such persons was called raff, riffraff, or trash.

In addition, there are several kinds of people who are both low-down and vicious. The kind we call a roughneck,

ROISTERERS

rowdy, or thug also was called a blisterer, brawler, hooligan, larrikin, plug-ugly, rip, roisterer, rough, ruffian, ruffler, scourer, or yap. A desperate criminal was a bravo, desperado, or *spadassin,* and a bully was a bangster, barrator, browbeater, buck, bulldozer, hector, and intimidator.

The Spenders

Neighbors used to be much more observant and critical of the way a man handled his financial affairs. They held an equally low opinion of those who spent too little, those who spent too much, and those who went out sponging and begging.

A spendthrift or squanderer was a prodigal (as the Prodigal Son), fribbler, fritterer, highflier, locust, rounder, spender, scattergood, or wastrell.

His opposite, the tightwad or miser, was called a cheeseparer, curmudgeon (also a cross, ill-natured person) , hunks, lickpenny, muckworm, niggard, nipcheese, pinchback, pinchfist, pinchpenny, scraper, screw, scrimp, skinflint, or snudge.

A greedy or grasping person was known as a coveter or harpy, a cheap individual was a cheapskate or tinhorn,

A PANHANDLER

A SNUFFLER

IMPLORERS

and, incidentally, a greedy eater was a cormorant, gobbler, gormand, gormandizer, gulper, guttler, or wolfer.

Beggars of alms or charity, who must have been relatively numerous in the old days, were called bacaches, badgemen, beadsmen, canters, fakirs, gaberlunzies, mumpers, mendicants, snufflers, panhandlers, randys, and schnorrers. Those who begged favors which might or might not have involved personal gain and, to the contrary, might have been actuated by the best of motives were known as adjurers, beseechers, entreators, implorers, importuners, or supplicators.

One who lived off others—a cadger or moocher—was called a sponge, parasite, trencher friend, or trencherman. The phrase, "he eats like a trencherman," means he eats greedily or heartily, as moochers so often do.

The Irresponsible Talkers

There have been dozens of names for people who abuse their power of speech in some way. For example, the teller of falsehoods—the liar—has been called an Ananias, equivocator, fabulist, falsifier, palterer, or prevaricator. If he tells small lies, he is a fibber or fibster.

One who carries tales to others—a tattletale—has been called many things, such as a blab, blabber, blabbermouth, pickthank, stag, talebearer, talecarrier, talemonger, taleteller, tattler, tittletattle, tittler, or snitch, the latter name also meaning thief.

An overly critical person—a scolder or reproacher—has been known as a berater, chider, clapperclawer, common scold, momus, railer, ranter, rater, reviler, slater, upbraider, or vituperator. Scolding used to be regarded as such a serious offense in colonial times that those found guilty of excessive criticism, usually women, were strapped in stools and ducked in a pond.

A quarrelsome individual has been known as a brabbler, brangler, bickerer, fire-eater, squabbler, or wrangler, and one given to whining is referred to as a bleater, puler, whimperer, or whiner. Anyone talking foolishness was called a blatherer, bleater, or gibberer.

An individual who shows scorn derisively—a scoffer—is a barracker, fleerer, flouter, girder, jeerer, jiber, scouter, sneerer, or shyer. Anyone who makes another person an object of laughter is a derider, mocker, rallier, ridiculer,

A COMMON SCOLD BEING DUCKED

taunt, taunter or twitter. A loud person or loud-mouth is a blatherskite, roarer, or stentor. Anyone given to violent denunciation is a curser, execrator, objurgator, or imprecator. A chronic faultfinder is a carper, caviler, or censurer.

One who makes injurious, evil statements about another is an asperser, backbiter, defamer, calumniator, libeler, maligner, missayer, slanderer, spatterer, splatterer, traducer, or villifier.

A bragger or boaster, a man who talks too big, is a blow, blower, blow-off, bouncer, braggadocio, braggart, fanfaron, gasconader, or vaporer. One who talks too much is a bag of wind, rattletrap, windbag, or windjammer, while one who chatters away incessantly is a babbler, chatterer, clatterer, chatterbox, claverer, crow, gabber, gabbler, gibblegabbler, jabberer, magpie, or prattler.

The Lickladles

A person who seeks to ingratiate himself with another by means of flattery was known as an adulator, beguiler, blandisher, cajoler, soother, or wheedler. If, on the contrary, he tried to draw others into danger by use of deception, he was a decoy or decoyer, enticer, inveigher, lurer, or seducer.

Another related practice that has always aroused contempt is that of bowing, scraping, and currying favor from others, as is shown by the names which have been applied to persons who so conduct themselves. Among the more polite of the names are apple-polisher and backscratcher.

Others include bootlicker, dog robber, fawn, fawner, lackey, lickdish, lickspit, lickfinger, lickfoot, lickladle, lickplatter,

A LICKDISH

lickspigot, parasite, spaniel, sycophant, toadeater, toady, truckler, and tufthunter.

The Unfortunate Women

There is an amazing number of uncomplimentary names for women in this age of chivalry. The kindest, meaning a flirt, is coquette. A silly girl is a goose, and a naive one is a ewelamb. An unkempt, untidy, often disreputable female is a dowdy, draggletail, frump, jade, malkin, scarecrow, slattern, sloven, tawpie, tit, trollop, or wallydrag. An ugly old woman is a carline, crone, hag, trot, or witch. If old and unmarried, she is a tabby, and if obese, she is a cow or sow. A boisterous, brawling, quarrelsome female is a barge, panther, shrew, tiger,

A GOOSE

A EWELAMB CONFESSING

termagant, vixen, virago, or wildcat.

There are numerous names for a woman of lowly status and easy virtue or no virtue at all. In addition to calling such a female a slut, floozie, or bitch, we have a choice of calling her a baggage, bawd, callet, cat, chippy, courtesan, demi-mondaine, demi-rep, doxy, drab, gillot, gillyflower, harridan, hooker, hustler, jezebel, mopsie, pug, punk, quean, rig, siren, skit, soiled dove, solicitor, strumpet, tart, tartlet, temptress, trull, wanton, and several other well-known names.

DRAGGLETAILS RECEIVING COMPANY

The Woman-Minded Men

When we speak of a man who has women on his mind, as many men have, we usually refer to him as a boy friend, a ladies' man, a wolf, a lecher, a trifler, or a petter, depending on our estimate of his interests, his intentions, and his techniques. But there are scores of other more colorful and more explicit names,

not all of them unfavorable, that we can use to enrich our conversations.

In place of boy friend, for example, we can use beau, spark, sparker, squire, steady, suitor, or, if he is countrified, swain.

For wolf, the man who likes to play around with girls but without real affection or serious intentions, we have such alternates as beguiler, charmer, coquet, flirt or flirter, masher, ogler, philanderer, or spooner.

Substitute names for the ladies' man who pays more serious attentions to the fair sex are amorist, cavalier, *cicisbeo*, chamberer, gallant, lovebird, lover, lover boy, lady killer, romancer, and woman chaser.

Then, to describe a man of strong sexual desire, we can use bull, boar, goat, ram, stud horse, or stallion, plus erotic and luster. A male who is swayed by his animal nature can be referred to as a beast, brute, sensualist, or voluptuary.

If our subject is a man of loose morals, there are such names as fancy man, lecher, paramour, libertine, punker, satyr, and wencher. Oddly enough, according to *Webster's*, a wench no longer is a naughty girl, a lewd woman or strumpet, because those definitions are

CRONES GOSSIPING

A SPARKER WITH HIS GIRL

archaic. Instead she now is: "a girl or maiden" or "girl of the peasant class; also, a female servant."

A man who toys with a woman's affections, leading her to believe that his intentions are more serious than they really are, is a trifler or frivoler.

A low-down male who attempts to lead a woman astray is a corrupter, debaucher or debauchee, decoyer, enslaver, ensnarer, enticer, inveigler, lurer, seducer, or tempter. If he goes about his seduction in a gay manner, he is a Lothario. If he carries her away phys-

ically, he is an abductor, ravisher, or transporter.

Next we come to the man who is known for his interest in amorous play. Depending on his techniques, he can be called a caresser, cosseter, cuddler, dallier, dandler, fondler, nestler, nuzzler, petter, player, smoocher, smoother, snoozler, snuggler, sporter, titillator, and so on.

If our ladies' man is the dissolute type, who leads a worthless life, he is a profligate, rake, rakehell, or roué, while if he is reckless and full of fire and spirit, he is called a blade, blood, hotspur, madcap, or spitfire.

Finally, a man who is merely fond of women is a philogynist, while one who hates them is a misogynist. One who hates marriage is a misogamist and, if he hates his children, a natural product of marriage, he is a misopedist. And a man who is taken in by a woman is a dupe, gull, fall guy, or sucker.

WOMAN-MINDED MEN

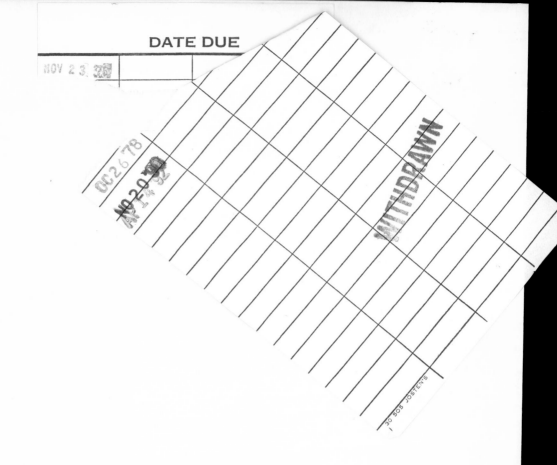